The indications are fascina
in the heart of an individual

and through his or her life. '₁ ___ ₃₃₃₃ descries an emerging expression of God's love in daily praying, caring, and sharing, moving the reader through the proven steps of love's cleansing, transforming, and empowering stages, initiated by a consistent outpouring of Jesus' Spirit. This tool will encourage the reader to first receive and then share God's love. Extraordinary encouragement comes from reading and responding to *40 Days of Love*.

> —TOM PHILLIPS, vice president, Billy Graham Evangelistic
> Association; executive director, Billy Graham Library

Years ago, I recall hearing lyrics that expressed the conviction that love isn't love until it's given away! *40 Days of Love: A Prayer, Care, Share Devotional* wonderfully captures the sentiment of that timeless idea. Here's a forty-day guide to help you experience Christ's love in remarkable new ways—and with plenty left over, give plenty away!

> —DICK EASTMAN, international president,
> Every Home for Christ

Have you ever wondered how to express the love of Christ to others in a way that could change their lives forever and impact the kingdom in significant ways? *40 Days of Love: A Prayer, Care, Share Devotional* is a compelling tool to teach you this lifestyle habit of praying for, caring about, and sharing the love of Jesus with neighbors, friends, and others. Allow yourself to be transformed and set on fire for the gospel as you live out His Great Commission of love through a Prayer-Care-Share lifestyle!

> —DAVE & KIM BUTTS, National Prayer Committee/
> Harvest Prayer Ministries

The church is relearning that the Great Commission will be fulfilled when Jesus' followers are daily obeying the Great Commandment: "As you go … make disciples … by loving God and loving your neighbor." This book partners with you to mobilize the men, women, students, and/or children you serve—to lead them into a daily practice that produces a lifestyle of love-motivated prayer, love-in-action care, and love-compelled sharing of the Good News of Jesus.

—PHIL MIGLIORATTI, Cityreaching.com
and Pray.Network

This book will help lead believers into a lifestyle of prayer, care for others, and sharing of Jesus with people by showing how important it is that we love others. If we don't feel loved by God, it is hard to share that love with other people. The next forty days will prepare you to receive His love so you can pass that on to others as a daily lifestyle.

—FORD TAYLOR, FSH Group/
Transformational Leadership

Inspiring, accessible, practical, and helpful—these takeaways will help you shape a Prayer-Care-Share lifestyle through which Jesus' Spirit will let you more beautifully help your family, neighbors, and friends touch the Lord's goodness of help, healing, and salvation. Branzell and Vennetti's book, *40 Days of Love: A Prayer, Care, Share Devotional*, will give you the daily equipping you need to live a Prayer-Care-Share lifestyle. You will not be sorry moving through this book as part of your daily worship walk with the Lord.

—REVEREND DR. BYRON SPRADLIN, president,
Artists in Christian Testimony International;
coordinator, Arts & Entertainment Affinity Group,
Mission America Coalition (Lausanne, USA)

In recent years, multitudes of Christians across the land have been praying for a nationwide awakening to Christ for all He is. Within this yeasty spiritual milieu, *40 Days of Love* calls us to action. Equal parts inspiration and implementation, here's a resource that will open your heart to Jesus and open your mouth for Jesus. An unbeatable combination!

—David Bryant, president, Proclaim Hope!;
author, *Christ Is ALL!*

Nothing will change our world more than accepting and then giving out the love of Jesus. Prepare yourself through this great read, and as you pray, let the Lord lead you forward every day with His love to change the world around you.

—Lisa Crump, chief operating officer,
National Day of Prayer Task Force

Kathy and Chris are two of my favorite people on the planet—because of their passion to help others live an authentic lifestyle of "Prayer, Care, and Share." Their new devotional will help us all to be on the journey—together.

—Tom Victor, president, The Great Commission Coalition;
facilitator, 4 to 14 Window North American Leadership Team;
executive team, International Prayer Council

What matters most to God about any Christian's life? Our Christlike character—that is, loving Him wholly and loving others selflessly. This dual outcome must be our daily prayer. It's how we show others that we care. It's the message that we share. Thank you, Chris V. and Kathy B., for devoting these meditations to those realities.

—Skip Garmo, PhD, Convener of Disciple Making in Mission America Coalition's "Love2020" Initiative; author, *The Leader's SEEcret: Asking the Right Questions & Embracing God's Answers*

Kathy Branzell and Chris Vennetti's *40 Days of Love: A Prayer, Care, Share Devotional* is a devotional tool that will help you in your personal prayer and devotional life. We all need tools to help us connect with the heart of God through prayer, and this tool is one of the best ever to do that. Start using this devotional each morning and you will immediately see a change in your spiritual life. I highly recommend this devotional if you want to improve your prayer life with God.

—Os Hillman, author, *TGIF: Today God Is First* and *The Joseph Calling*

True love is always revolutionary! Those who came in contact with the early Christians were bowled over by the love of God radiating through their words and actions. They turned the world upside down! This practical 40 Days of Love guide will have the same revolutionary impact on you, your church members, and your community. Get it, read it, and implement it for transformational breakthrough where you live!

—John Robb, International Prayer Council, World Prayer Assembly, National Prayer Assembly (USA)

In our world filled with so much hate and confusion, Christ followers need to be experiencing the love of Christ themselves and expressing it to our broken world. Reading this book and learning from these two kingdom-minded leaders will launch you into living a Prayer-Care-Share lifestyle that impacts your friends and even your whole community!

—Mark Slaughter, evangelist, InterVarsity Christian Fellowship; National Facilitator of Emerging Generations, Mission America Coalition

I pray that everyone reads *40 Days of Love*! It will bless you and equip you to enjoy a Prayer-Care-Share lifestyle.

—PAUL CEDAR, chairman, Mission America Coalition

In Acts 1:8, Christ told the disciples to *be* witnesses, not *do* witnessing. This forty-day journey with Jesus comes from the hearts of two Christ followers who have learned the art of "being." I encourage you to join them in this forty-day commitment to knowing Christ and making Him known.

—REV. GARY FROST, National Facilitator for Prayer,
Mission America Coalition

Love changes everything and everyone. Kindness is God's gift and instrument of mercy to mankind. *40 Days of Love* is a daily devotional that will deeply challenge you live out God's lovingkindness toward others around you. Join the adventure of the Prayer-Care-Share lifestyle. It will change your life!

—MILTON MONELL, Director of Global Prayer
for Campus Crusade for Christ, Int'l

Chris Vennetti and Kathy Branzell have penned a practical guide to demonstrating God's love to a hurting world in *40 Days of Love: A Prayer, Care, Share Devotional*. Step one: They guide you to experience the love of Christ personally through well-chosen Scripture passages coupled with key insights. Step two: They offer probing questions to prepare yourself to act purely. Step three: They suggest doable prompts to love others. If embracing the Prayer-Care-Share lifestyle is a step out of your comfort zone, don't worry. This devotional is a gentle arm around you to lead the way.

—JULIE LOOS, Ratio Christi, Director of Prayer and Outreach;
Moms in Prayer International, College Groups Facilitator

As a member of the Mission America Coalition for over twenty years, I still need constant encouragement to practice a Prayer-Care-Share lifestyle in my own life and neighborhood. Chris and Kathy have definitely encouraged me through their own personal commitment to this vision, and anything they write will get my attention and help me grow my own witness. I recommend this book to you for the same reasons, and trust that together we will see many respond in faith.

—JOHN QUAM

In a world where love has "grown cold," the Holy Spirit can use this forty-day journey to rekindle the much-needed testimony of His love. As His church has too often been led astray from the simplicity and purity of devotion to Christ, these forty days can restore us to Great Commission living, empowered by Great Commandment love.

—DR. DAVID FERGUSON, co-chair,
Awakening America Alliance

BroadStreet Publishing® Group, LLC
Racine, Wisconsin, USA
BroadStreetPublishing.com

40 DAYS of **LOVE:** A PRAYER, CARE, SHARE Devotional

Copyright © 2017 Chris Vennetti and Kathy Branzell

ISBN-13: 978-1-4245-5522-2 (softcover)
ISBN-13: 978-1-4245-5534-5 (e-book)

All rights reserved. No part of this book may be reproduced in any form, except for brief quotations in printed reviews, without permission in writing from the publisher.

Unless otherwise noted, all Scripture quotations are from *The Holy Bible, English Standard Version*. Copyright © 2000; 2001 by Crossway Bibles, a division of Good News Publishers. Used by permission. All rights reserved Scripture quotations marked NASB are taken from the *New American Standard Bible*, © Copyright 1960, 1962, 1963, 1968, 1971, 1972, 1973, 1975, 1977 by The Lockman Foundation. Used by permission. Scripture quotations marked NIV are taken from the Holy Bible, New International Version®, NIV® Copyright ©1973, 1978, 1984, 2011 by Biblica, Inc.® Used by permission. All rights reserved worldwide.

Stock or custom editions of BroadStreet Publishing titles may be purchased in bulk for educational, business, ministry, fundraising, or sales promotional use. For information, please email info@broadstreetpublishing.com.

Cover by Garborg Design
Interior design and typesetting by Katherine Lloyd at theDESKonline.com

Printed in the United States of America

17 18 19 20 21 5 4 3 2 1

Contents

Section Four: Spiritual Keys to Remain in God's Love

Section Five: The Fruit of God's Love

Introduction

*So now faith, hope, and love abide, these three; but the
greatest of these is love.*

1 Corinthians 13:13

I t is safe to say that every heart on planet Earth longs to know
God's love. As Paul writes here, when all is said and done, faith,
hope, and love will remain, but the greatest is love. Jesus Himself
stated that love for God and love for others are the most important things. Therefore, we believe taking forty days to experience
God's love for us, and then learning how He intends for us to
express this love to others, is one of the greatest time investments
we could ever make.

We are so excited to go on this journey with you into the
heart of God's great love. It is hard to think of a more exciting and
more important topic than love. It is our hope and prayer that,
as you move through each day's devotional, you will be inspired
to receive and experience God's love at a depth you have never
known. Each day we will also provide a practical opportunity to
express the love of God to others through Prayer, Care, and Share
action points.

Take some time now to write down the names of ten people you will pray for over the next forty days, and pray for them
every day. Write down ten names of people you want to show
Christlike care, and finally write down ten names of people you

would like to share the gospel message of Jesus with over the next forty days.[1] The Holy Spirit will prompt you with other names as you go through these devotionals and will provide you with many opportunities to show and share the love of Jesus with friends, family, and complete strangers. Remain watchful and available.

There are two main sections to each day's reading: Experience God's Love (written by Chris) and Express God's Love (from Kathy). As you move through the devotional, be sensitive to items that God's Spirit is highlighting to you. Take time to wait on Him rather than rush through the Prayer, Care, Share action points. If something stands out, mark the book, or keep a separate journal where you can document what God is speaking. As you follow His lead, we trust He will take various facets of this book and use them to mold you into His image. As you join Him in praying through what He shows you, and as you make the necessary lifestyle adjustments, we trust that you will experience a true transformation taking place.

It is our joy and pleasure to be with you on this forty-day journey. Be prepared to experience and express the love of God as you never have before!

Learning to love with you,

Chris Vennetti & Kathy Branzell

For more information on participating with the 40 Days of Love, go to: 40DaysofLove.net or visit Love2020.com.

---

1 We have a sample "Prayer, Care, Share" brochure in association with the *40 Days of Love* that you could use for this opportunity. You can find it at http://www. 40daysoflove.net/wp-content/PDF/40daysoflove_inside.pdf.

Section One

PREPARING OUR HEARTS TO LOVE

It is my prayer that your love may abound more and more, with knowledge and all discernment, so that you may approve what is excellent, and so be pure and blameless for the day of Christ.

Philippians 1:9–10

We are called to a life of abounding love. Is that how you would classify your current level of love in the relationships that God has entrusted to you? Are you living a pure and blameless life that prefers others above yourself? If you are like many sincere followers of Christ, we can know these things are supposed to be true of us, yet fail to walk in them as our daily reality.

As we begin this journey into God's love, it will be helpful to define exactly what God means by *love* and to see where we are in experiencing and expressing His love. In 2 Corinthians, Paul encourages us to "examine" ourselves (2 Corinthians 13:5). Where do you stand in relationship to a life that is fully surrendered to God? Have you been walking out a lifestyle of complete trust in Him, or does your heart still doubt His unwavering love?

This first section of devotionals is a personal preparation of the heart as you begin to think and prepare to care and share God's love through personal and corporate acts of love. Take these days to be filled with His love and then let it begin to spill out all over your community—over your home, neighborhood, church, work, school, and wherever else God leads you. You cannot express what you have not experienced first; be faithful to spend these first days soaking in the love of your Savior. We hope that by the time you complete these first ten days, you will have fully surrendered your life to Jesus Christ. We hope that you will have entered more fully into trusting God with every aspect of your life. As we enter this time of heart preparation, let's pray:

Father, I thank you that you desire me to live in a place of total abandonment to your great love. You desire for me to trust your love completely so that I will never doubt you. Today, I believe you will encounter me with your love, and I thank you in advance for how you are going to prepare my heart to be an instrument of love to all those you allow into my life.

Let's be prepared to love well!

What Is Love?

Love is patient and kind; love does not envy or boast; it is not arrogant or rude. It does not insist on its own way; it is not irritable or resentful; it does not rejoice at wrongdoing, but rejoices with the truth. Love bears all things, believes all things, hopes all things, endures all things.

1 Corinthians 13:4–7

EXPERIENCE GOD'S LOVE

The Word of God unfolds an unselfish love that cares more for others than we care for ourselves. However, popular culture uses the word *love* to mean many different things. Take for instance the following examples:

A young girl with candy dripping down her chin declares, "I *love* chocolate."

A grown man jumps up from his courtside seat and shouts, "I *love* this team!"

A high school student encourages his girlfriend to get an abortion as he whispers, "I really *love* you, and I don't want anything to come between us."

Expressions like these should make us wonder what exactly we are talking about when we use the word *love*. Is all love the same, or are there variations that we should be aware of?

The ancient Greeks came up with multiple words to express different types of love. This is not an exhaustive list, but three words that they used to define love were *eros*, *philia*, and *agape*.

Eros is where we get the word *erotic*. It refers to a passionate physical attraction in which our motives are often about what we can get out of the relationship. *Philia* is the type of emotional love you have for a brother or sister. The Greek word *agape* refers to an unconditional love. It is love that gives without expecting anything in return, a love that moves us to action no matter what the cost may be to ourselves. It is this love that motivated Jesus to go to the cross so that sinful humanity could be saved. This type of love is a choice.

Aren't you glad that God's love for you is of the agape variety? His love for you is patient and kind. He is not frustrated or irritated. He bears all things, believes all things, hopes all things, and endures all things. His love for you is beyond what your human mind can even comprehend. Yet it is as real and consistent as the rising and setting of the sun.

Only as we come to know the depth of love that God has for us will we be able to give that same type of love to others.

Father, I ask that you show me your love. I admit that my understanding of love falls far short of what you intended. As I take the next forty days to experience your love, I ask that your Holy Spirit would fill me with the reality of unconditional love. I thank you for this in advance right now. (Continue to pray as God's Spirit leads you.)

EXPRESS GOD'S LOVE

Let Christ's love wash over you and fill you as you ponder the depths and dimensions of His love for you. It is only in that love that the Spirit equips you to express love. You learn to love others through the love we experience from Christ. For example, when you realize how patient God is with you, it humbles you to be patient with others. The Holy Spirit prompts you toward affections, attitudes, and actions of love that lifts up, forgive freely, and bring courage and hope into the life of another.

👤 **Prayer:** *Lord, thank you for loving me so deeply, so perfectly, and so patiently. Fill me with your love so that it overflows my heart and pours out through my speech and my steps. Let all that I say and do be a reflection of your love for me. Please put people on my mind and in my path that need to be loved today. Holy Spirit, equip me with love as I express what I experience in you. Now I pray that* _____ (insert the name of someone you are praying for) *would experience your love, as they need you to bear* _____ (insert a circumstance or trial they are going through). *I pray they would fully believe in you and your Word, and know that you are our hope in all things.* (Pray for those on your prayer list.)

💜 **Care:** Prepare and commit to express the attributes of love today and always. What will patience look like when you are inconvenienced or someone does not act or react as you would like them to? How will your kindness help shield or sustain someone through the cruelty of a selfish culture? Find ways to shine the spotlight of credit and appreciation on others even if you could boast in an accomplishment. Check your mood; determine to make your presence add life and joy to a room.

♻ **Share:** It is a misnomer to think that trials and troubles cease when you become a Christian; the truth is that Jesus will cover you as the Holy Spirit guards and guides you *through* the tough times, not around them. Someone you know or that you will meet today needs to know the attributes of God's love for them and what it looks like to express this love to others. Be prepared to share and show love.

The Source
of All Real Love

Anyone who does not love does not know God, because God is love.

1 John 4:8

EXPERIENCE GOD'S LOVE

Love is a person. When we realize this, we see that our desire to be loved is really a desire to know God. This simplifies everything. Now, instead of feeling like we have to chase after dozens of people, places, or things to make us happy, we need only one pursuit. The pursuit of knowing and being known by God, the source of love.

The truth is, our souls are all longing for a garden experience. The kind of love and intimacy that Adam and Eve had with God before the fall. Amazingly enough, through the death, resurrection, and ascension of Jesus, the way has now been paved for this to become our daily reality. There is no hindrance or lack of desire on God's end of this relationship. What remains to be seen is if we will choose to seek Him until we begin to tap more deeply into His life.

If you have the opportunity to go to the Nile River, it is well worth the trip. I can assure you that virtually no one looks out at that body of flowing water and thinks to themselves, *I wonder if this water is going to run out today?* The Nile River, which has been flowing unbroken across the continent of Africa for thousands of years, is a visual picture of the unending flow of love that pours from God to each and every one of us.

Simply go to the source today and drink deeply of Him. His love for you will never run dry. "Come to me, all who labor and are heavy laden, and I will give you rest" (Matthew 11:28).

Father, I ask for your forgiveness for the times that I have sought to find love and satisfaction apart from you. Today, I choose to turn to you as my only source of real contentment. I choose to believe that as I seek you first, every other need I have will be satisfied. Thank you for filling me to overflowing today.

EXPRESS GOD'S LOVE

God is love. This statement is the foundation of love; it describes who God is and that His thoughts, plans, and actions toward us are bathed in His love. It is difficult to understand when we see suffering around us. We often hear people say, "How could a loving God allow … ?" Remember that Jesus said, "In the world you will have tribulation. But take heart; I have overcome the world" (John 16:33). We will not fully understand many things on this side of heaven, but love is the foundation of knowing God and should frame every thought and emotion we have toward Him and others. If we claim to know and experience Him, then the proof will be in the love we express toward Him and others. His is a love we cannot selfishly claim and contain, but a love that flows freely through us like the Nile through Africa.

Prayer: Lord, let your love surge through me today like a rushing river. I want people to recognize your love in me and to receive a touch of your love through me. Let my words and actions be evidence of our relationship—not just my knowing you but loving you.

Care: Many people are looking for evidence that God really exists. Apologetics offer evidence for those who need head knowledge and "proof" of Jesus and biblical people, places, and stories, but the message first comes through the heart. God draws men's hearts to Himself; we have a longing, a hole in our heart that only He can fill. People need to hear and see the evidence of God in your words and deeds before they will consider the "unseen." What will they see in you today and over these forty days? Begin planning and taking action in big and small ways to share the God of true love.

⛅ **Share:** When you value others with acts of compassion, you will stand out in a selfish world and people will be curious about the reason you have hope. It is necessary to share the reason for your hope, to let people know that Christ's love for you and your love for Him is the source and strength for all that you do. Do not let people label you as just a "do-gooder," but rather "God's doer."

Staying Connected to the Source

"Abide in me, and I in you. As the branch cannot bear fruit by itself, unless it abides in the vine, neither can you, unless you abide in me. I am the vine; you are the branches. Whoever abides in me and I in him, he it is that bears much fruit, for apart from me you can do nothing."

John 15:4–5

EXPERIENCE GOD'S LOVE

One time, when I (Chris) was meditating on the importance of staying connected to God, I saw a visual picture of a scuba diver. The diver was swimming so deep that there was no way he could possibly make it back to the surface in time to get air if he lost his mask. I then saw the diver bump against a coral reef, and his air tank got tangled and knocked off his back. His mask and air tank started falling toward the bottom of the ocean. The thought came to my mind, *If that were me, how desperate would I be to reach the tank and put the air mask back on?* Obviously, I would stop everything else and do whatever it took to regain the tank and secure the mask before I died. God's Spirit then whispered to my heart, "You should regard your connection to me with the same sense of urgency that this diver would his mask."

How many of us treat our connection to God as a casual thing? If it requires some level of self-sacrifice to take time in the Word of God, prayer, or worship, to remain connected to Him, how many of us hit the snooze button, thinking nothing of it? How many of us neglect a deep level of relationship, in which we are honest about where we are really at with the Lord, with other believers? As those who have been called out of the world to be children of God and His royal ambassadors to the world, we cannot afford a haphazard treatment of our connection to God.

May our heart cry become, "Whatever it takes. Whatever the sacrifice. I am willing."

The Spirit of God is our spiritual air. We cannot survive, let alone thrive, without Him.

Father, I ask for your forgiveness for times when I have neglected our connection. I am sorry for counting other things as more important than our relationship. By your grace, I believe you to fill me with a sense of spiritual urgency to always maintain a deep connection to you no matter what it takes.

EXPRESS GOD'S LOVE

To "abide" is a continual action of being held by, attached to, or kept in place near your source and means of survival. Abiding as branches in the vine of Jesus means we allow Him to hold us, surround us, and pour lessons through us so that we can thrive during times of "pestilence" and the "pruning" that make us even more fruitful. It is in abiding that we experience Christ's love and the fruit of the Spirit in and through our lives. Apart from Him we cannot express real love. Abiding in Him we are sourced to love even in the most difficult of circumstances.

👤 **Prayer:** Lord, thank you for pouring your love through me like life-giving sap runs through a vine. I am thankful to be a branch on your vine. Please prompt and protect me as the world pulls at me with distractions or discouragement. Hold me close as you examine me, and prune me with discipline and discipleship that I might bear more fruit for your glory. Please help me to wait on you and to grow in the direction that you steer and stake me to go. Use me to support others who are growing in their knowledge and love for you.

❤ **Care:** Have you ever noticed how a vine grows with its branches intertwined, adding additional support to each branch as it matures and produces fruit? God puts people in your life so that you can grow together and support one another through storms and tender places of new growth. Who do you know that could use some extra support right now? There are many ways to provide support: through prayer; spending time listening and encouraging; providing a meal, a ride to an appointment, or childcare for a few hours; or completing an errand or chore, etc. Take time as part of the vine today.

⌂ **Share:** In Scripture we are prompted to abide in Christ and His love, and to let His Word (Scripture) abide in us. It is important to be prepared to give a reason for the hope we have when someone asks (1 Peter 3:15). So what is your story of God's glory in you? Be prepared to share what Christ means to you as well as what He has done in you, and for you, as you walk and work in a world of hurting people who need hope today.

The Great Exchange

I have been crucified with Christ. It is no longer I who live, but Christ who lives in me. And the life I now live in the flesh I live by faith in the Son of God, who loved me and gave himself for me.

Galatians 2:20

EXPERIENCE GOD'S LOVE

Paul makes an amazing statement here. He says that his corrupt nature, which was the root of his sin, has been killed in Christ's death, and that he literally no longer lives. He says that the life that is lived through him is a life of faith in which the Spirit of Jesus actually lives His life on Paul's behalf. Has this been your experience of the Christian life? Have you truly learned to count your selfish nature as dead, and in turn live exclusively by the power of the Holy Spirit?

Since it is clear that this is God's desire for every one of His children, we would be wise to meditate on the truth that Paul is presenting here until this becomes our daily reality. We can know that God does not show partiality. What He promises in the Scriptures to one of us, He promises to all.

Jesus offers to live His life on our behalf. What a glorious offer! Our sinful, selfish, broken, fallen, finite lives that can bear no lasting fruit for God's kingdom can be exchanged for the perfect, infinite, overcoming, and fruit-filled life of God Himself. In Christian theology, this has often been called "The Great Exchange."

Indeed, it is a great exchange. We give Jesus all of our life. He gives us all of His life. Not just as a someday, faraway intellectual concept, but as a living, breathing reality right here and now! The truth is, if we could see the eternal life that Jesus is offering us this very moment, we would all make this complete exchange as quickly as possible.

Our hesitancy is based on our deception—either in believing that the life we have apart from Christ is somehow worth holding on to, or that the life Christ is offering us is deficient in some way and will leave us unsatisfied.

Nothing could be farther from the truth. The life offered to us by the Spirit of God is nothing short of heaven on earth. This is the life mankind was created for since the beginning of time. Only as we enter more deeply into the reality of exchanging our lives for the life of Christ will we come to know real fulfillment. Make this exchange today, then allow God's Spirit to teach you how to live an exchanged life every day.

Father, I ask for your forgiveness for the many times that I have held on to my life and not trusted you to live your life in and through me. Today, I choose to fully exchange my self-led life for your glorious eternal life. Thank you for making this exchanged life available to me!

EXPRESS GOD'S LOVE

We often think of surrender as a loss, but in Christ, surrender means victory! As we surrender flesh to faith and earthly to eternal, there is great gain as we receive something more valuable and beneficial than we could have ever imagined. Surrender empties us of self and fills us with the Spirit; it makes space for supernatural things to happen in us and through us. Surrender gives us open eyes to see opportunities and others as God sees them and open hands to give and receive God's best.

Prayer: Lord, I surrender all—every thought, desire, and area of my life. I want to live by faith, not flesh. I want your victory to fill my life, to enable me to share your love and message with everyone by the way I treat them, the things I say to them, and the expressions of my faith in you alone. Thank you for giving me life, life in you. I want the people on my prayer list (name them) to have life in you.

Care: People often need a hand of flesh to hold on to as they reach for Jesus. It is one thing to prompt someone to let go of earthly thoughts and sin-filled desires, but when they open their hand to release the hurtful things, they need to feel the support of someone helpful. People need people. People suffering from addiction, or those who are tempted to commit a crime for money so they can buy diapers for their children, or those who need to reject the wrong type of relationship because they desire attention and love, are just a few examples of people who need someone to journey with them from flesh to faith. Who do you know that could use your caring hand and heart to help guide them toward victory today?

⛅ Share: This world appears to have a lot to offer; choices compete for our attention, time, and money. We fill our days and our closets searching for satisfaction and significance. Some decisions quickly turn into regret, and "buyer's remorse" sets in to steal the joy of the new toy. Do you know someone drowning in regret or disappointment? There is a world of people searching for fulfillment; share with them the story of surrender, and walk with them as Jesus fills their life with real treasure.

To Love God
Is to Obey God

"As the Father has loved me, so have I loved you. Abide in my love. If you keep my commandments, you will abide in my love, just as I have kept my Father's commandments and abide in his love."

John 15:9–10

EXPERIENCE GOD'S LOVE

Jesus said to love Him is to obey Him. Western society has given us so many definitions for love, but most of them are related to our emotions. Very few of us think of loving God as obedience or submission to Him. We can only understand this when we come to realize the biblical meaning of the word *love*. The original Greek word for love is transliterated *agapao*, and it means to "actively do what the Lord prefers."[2] So, to love God is to prefer Him above yourself. Having this understanding of love is critical and has wide-ranging implications.

When we say, "I love God," we are not merely saying that we have a fond emotional affection for God. We are saying that in

2   James Strong, *Strong's Exhaustive Concordance of the Bible* (Nashville: Thomas Nelson, 2009), s.v. "agapao," http://biblehub.com/greek/25.htm (accessed April 9, 2017).

all circumstances, by the empowerment given to us by His Holy Spirit, we will choose His will above our own.

Jesus modeled this preference of His Father's will for us in the garden of Gethsemane prior to His crucifixion. He preferred His Father's will above His own. "Father, if you are willing, remove this cup from me. Nevertheless, not my will, but yours, be done" (Luke 22:42).

To love God means that we agree to put the whole of our lives in complete submission to another person who we are acknowledging is so far greater than us, that He is worthy of our complete adoration in every facet of our lives.

Likewise, to say that you love another human being is not a small matter. Before we casually use the words, "I love you," we would be wise to first check our hearts and ask ourselves, *Am I really living in a way that shows that I care more about this person than I care about myself?* If not, then rather than using vain words, may we ask God's Spirit to teach us to care more about others than we care about ourselves. When our words and actions go hand in hand, we can expect the love of God expressed through us to produce powerful results.

Father, today I choose to express my love for you by preferring your will and your ways above my own. Help me to understand the implications of what it means to truly love you with the whole of my life. I desire to remain in your love, and I choose to believe you will give me the spiritual strength I need to prefer you at all times and in every circumstance.

EXPRESS GOD'S LOVE

We often do not equate love with obedience. Depending on your background and experiences, you may think of obedience as something you do begrudgingly to avoid punishment, or something mandatory out of respect for authority or rank. What thoughts come to mind when you think of obedience? Now let me ask you: How do you feel when you are obeyed? Do you feel appreciated and respected? Jesus said in John 14:23 that if we love Him, we will obey Him. In the family of God, obedience flows from a heart that seeks to delight the one who gives life. Obedience is a love-filled response to Christ's love for you.

● Prayer: Lord, I seek to obey your will, your Word, and your ways because I love you deeply. I know that my works are useless outside of your will and Spirit. I cannot earn my way into your kingdom, nor do my acts make you love me more or less. I obey in a response to your love and in respect for you as my God.

♥ Care: Have you ever been prompted to do something for someone that had hurt you or that you struggled to be around? Have you ever felt God nudging you to do something for someone that was an inconvenience for you, that you did not think they deserved, or that you thought they wouldn't appreciate your efforts? Have you ever had your heart hurt for someone in need but refused to be generous toward them because of how they might spend or use your gift? Understand that your only responsibility is to obey God's opportunity; how they respond is between God and them. You are sowing a seed, nurturing spiritual growth, maybe even answering a prayer. If you have not been obedient to God in any way, go and be obedient today.

⌂ **Share:** Your joy-filled obedience can be a significant testimony to help others take the first step in trusting and obeying Jesus. Resentful obedience reflects a heart that does not understand the better blessings found in the boundaries and promptings of God. Pride says, "I want what I want, no matter the consequences." Obedience says and shows the world that you trust God to give you what you need and to shield you from what you do not. Be prepared to share this message with someone today and every day.

Day 6

Love Awakens Faith

*So we have come to know and to believe the love that God
has for us. God is love, and whoever abides in love abides in
God, and God abides in him.*

1 John 4:16

EXPERIENCE GOD'S LOVE

Janice was a young girl with a physical disability. Growing up in
the mountains of Colorado, she wanted to learn to ride a bike.
Her father was determined that she would be able to do this and
put lots of time into training her. As Janice attempted to pedal
and pick up speed, she would get tired and her bike would start to
tip over. Each time she was falling, her father attempted to catch
her and encourage her: "You can do this! Together we will see it
happen!"

Years later, with a silver medal around her neck at the Special
Olympics, Janice searched for her father in the stands. He was
still there, cheering her on with a handwritten sign: "Janice is
LOVED!"

Do you think Janice trusts her father? Without a doubt. In
the same way, when we come to know and believe the love that
God has for us, we too will learn to trust Him. Without a doubt.

When we come to know and believe the love that God has for

us, something happens in our heart. A confidence begins to rise up. We can do this. With His help and His indwelling Holy Spirit, nothing is impossible for us. Knowing God's love for us is like a key that unlocks an untold number of spiritual treasures.

Do you know that God loves you? (Take a moment to really reflect on this.)

Ask God, "Right now, would you begin to reveal to me the love that you have for me?" (Take enough time to wait and allow His Spirit to speak to you.)

Like Janice, we all need to know that our Father God is for us and not against us, that He has our best interest at heart. The truth is, our heavenly Father is a much greater encourager than Janice's father ever could be. He loves us perfectly at all times. He will never leave us or forsake us. Trust His love for you today. Allow His love to awaken a renewed faith in your heart that nothing is impossible with His assistance.

The obstacles you see in your life today can become the testimonies to God's faithfulness that you stand on tomorrow.

Father God, I ask that you bring me to a place of faith in which I know that I know that you love me with your whole heart. May the love that you have for me awaken a deep faith in my heart that cannot be shaken no matter what is going on around me. I thank you even now for this revelation of your love for me.

EXPRESS GOD'S LOVE

We tend to become what we abide in; the habits and character of where we grew up and the people and places we spend our time with now tend to affect our personality and behavior. It is not just a "birds of a feather flock together" mentality. We really do have the power to shape the atmosphere where we live, work, worship, and learn. Even a smile on your face can cause someone to smile—try it all day and see what happens. Abiding in God's love saturates you with love that will spill out of your life and all over the people around you.

Prayer: Lord, thank you for your deep abiding love for me. Thank you for surrounding and supporting me with your love and then sending me to share it. I want to abide in your love that provides love for others. I want my life to be a fountain of your flowing love, and as I experience it, I want to express it back to you and others.

Care: Love is a verb. It is more than a feeling; it has feet that go and fingers that do. Love is expressed even before you feel it; love moves in faith believing that what God has demonstrated toward us, we are commissioned to share with others. Love stands out in a world of selfishness and hate. Determine now how you will love well today. Stand out by going out of your way to be kind and serve others. When others are cruel, be kind. Where there is selfishness, be selfless. Abide but don't hide in His love.

⛅ **Share:** We are storytellers by design. For thousands of years, people have been passing down history and stories in the oral tradition. Even after printing presses and laptops, we still love a good conversation filled with life's adventures and emotions. You share stories all the time whether you realize it or not, so make it a habit to share God stories in your everyday conversations. Give Him glory for the great things He has done, or connect a current life situation with a story from the Bible to open the door to faith discussions or questions from unbelievers. Let them know they can talk to you without judgment or pressure. Always have transparent, real-life conversations, and avoid "church language" they may not understand.

We Can Trust God's Love Wholeheartedly

Trust in the LORD with all your heart, and do not lean on your own understanding. In all your ways acknowledge him, and he will make straight your paths.

Proverbs 3:5–6

EXPERIENCE GOD'S LOVE

Isn't it a wonderful thing to know that God loves us? When we have a revelation of just how much God loves us, then trust comes easily. When we realize that there is someone who has unlimited power and infinite knowledge, and who always has our best interests at heart, how difficult should it be for us to trust Him? The Word of God says that when we discard our limited human understanding related to the people and circumstances that surround us, and instead entrust ourselves completely into the hands of God, He will make our paths straight.

The original Hebrew word for *straight* here is transliterated *yashar* and refers to making our steps smooth, right, directed, and agreeable.[3] Who wouldn't want the decisions we make to be

---

3 Strong, *Strong's Exhaustive Concordance of the Bible*, s.v. "yashar," http://biblehub .com/hebrew/3474.htm (accessed April 9, 2017).

directed by a person who is all-knowing? Who wouldn't want a smooth and agreeable course of life? All that is required is that we step beyond our limited human understanding and into the supernatural.

Trusting God is easy. You might say, "Well, that hasn't been my experience." Then I (Chris) would reply, "Then you need a deeper revelation of His great love for you." As you come to know His love, not merely intellectually or as a past experience, but as a living, breathing reality in the here and now, trust comes simply. Like a child.

The love of God expressed toward us, not merely two thousand years ago on the cross, but right here this moment as you read these words, should make trust a simple thing. Trusting God should be the easiest part of our day. He has earned our trust, He is worthy of it, and even in the areas that we may not understand, He calls to us, "Cast aside your understanding and trust me, I will take care of the rest!"

Father, I thank you for always being faithful. I thank you that you are the one person whom I can trust at all times and never doubt that you have my best interests at heart. Today, I choose to trust you completely with everything that concerns me. I know that you will guide my steps and make my paths straight. I love you and I trust you.

EXPRESS GOD'S LOVE

Trust is a big word—it means to feel safe, to be bold, confident, and secure. It seems like trust would be easy when it is attached to God: Creator of the universe, all-knowing, all-seeing, mighty, faithful, the one who is love. How could you not trust Him, right? It seems easy until the diagnosis, the financial crisis, or the crumbling relationship. How do you respond then? The answer is in the rest of the verse: don't rest on the support of what you see in your situation or lean on your own learning. Trust comes from your experiences with God. We walk in the confidence of His wisdom, not what we can assess in our surroundings. He loves us and levels out our path when we boldly believe and take His hand to journey through the situations to the solutions.

👤 **Prayer:** Lord, you are wisdom—you know and see everything from beginning to end. Help me to be courageous and confident because I abide in the love of Christ. Remind me to acknowledge you, to seek your will, your wisdom, and the foundation of your faithfulness in my life in all my ways and decisions. Let me walk in your ways, under the shelter of your wings, where I find comfort even when my world seems to swirl in chaos.

♥ **Care:** One of my favorite new sayings is, "We move at the speed of trust." Trust is not built overnight. It can be destroyed in a minute, but it takes time to build and strengthen. It grows though shared experiences, confidences maintained, proven reliability, no deceitful agendas or selfish ambitions, and knowing someone has your back and your best interests at heart. Who have you built that kind of relationship with in your lifetime? How could you begin building that relationship with people around you who need a trusted friend? If you have ever broken trust, take responsibility, apologize, and begin to earn it back.

⛅ **Share:** Life is full of surprises, good and bad. As you walk and work through your day today, you will pass by dozens of people who have been shocked and rocked by unexpected, painful circumstances. How can you share the love and message of Jesus with them now? How can you give them a hand out of the pit they fell (or got pushed) into? Share your trust in Jesus, the one they can always trust.

Called to Forgive

*"Forgive us our debts, as we also have forgiven our debtors.
... For if you forgive others their trespasses, your heavenly
Father will also forgive you, but if you do not forgive others their trespasses, neither will your Father forgive your
trespasses."*

Matthew 6:12, 14–15

EXPERIENCE GOD'S LOVE

Tears are often an indicator of physical or emotional pain. Pain
hurts. God's intention in allowing us to walk through pain is
always good, though we often cannot see this at the time. It helps
to be aware that the greatest goal He has in His heart for His
children is that we will be conformed into the image of His Son,
Jesus. Sometimes, in the midst of our pain, just knowing these
truths in our minds is not enough to comfort us.

What about the times when those closest to you caused you
the most pain due to their words or actions? What about the
times that those you looked up to, or those who were even leaders
in the church, failed you? What about when all hell breaks loose
and you feel like you have no one you can turn to who understands or cares? What then?

A simple yet profound prescription arises from the Word of

God. It is completely counterintuitive to our natural minds, and yet, because God has told us it is the solution, it is in fact the only thing that works. Forgiveness. Letting go. Choosing to cancel the debt we believe we are owed by our offender and entrusting justice entirely to the judge of all the earth.

Easy? No. Possible? Yes, through the empowerment given to us by the Holy Spirit. Keep in mind that the same Spirit that lived inside of Jesus, and was able to forgive His murderers while He was suffocating on the cross, lives inside of you. The same Holy Spirit who gave Stephen the grace to forgive his murderers while stones were crushing his body, lives inside of you (Acts 7:60). This is not a matter of mustering up enough human strength. This is a matter of humbling ourselves before the Spirit of God and asking Him to give us the grace to forgive.

> *Father, I ask for your forgiveness for the ways that I have wrongfully responded to those who have sinned against me. Today, I choose as an act of my will to forgive* _____ (name of your offender) *for the way that he/she has sinned against me:* _____ (be as specific as you can here). *By the power of the Holy Spirit, I cancel* _____ (offender's name) *debt once and for all, and I choose to ask that you bless* _____ (offender's name) *by molding him/her into your image. By your grace, I choose to no longer speak about the offense against me but instead to speak blessings over* _____ (offender's name). *I trust you to protect and defend me. I believe you to heal my heart of this offense now so that I may love well.*

EXPRESS GOD'S LOVE

Have you ever had to ask for forgiveness? It is the step that comes right after you apologize. Forgiveness asks God and others to wipe away the incident, to refrain from holding it against you as you take steps to heal the wound or earn the affection or trust back. Forgiveness gives up the right to get even; it releases the debt and leaves it behind as you move forward. Carrying unforgiveness in our lives often hurts us more than the person we won't forgive. It is like drinking poison and expecting the other person to die. It is decay in our soul and hurt in our heart. Jesus instructs us to forgive as God has forgiven us; our sin is wiped away, as far as the east is from the west, washed clean and not counted against us. If God can forgive me, who am I to hold a grudge?

Prayer: Thank you, Lord, for your forgiveness; for paying the penalty for my sin and covering me with your righteousness. Let my heart forgive the way you have forgiven me, fully and freely. Prompt me where I have not asked for your forgiveness or where I need to be forgiven by another. Let your forgiveness mark my path with humility and gentleness toward others, making me quick to forgive.

Care: When typing the word *unforgiveness* on a computer, a red zigzag line shows up, prompting that it is not a word; autocorrect suggests changing it to *forgiveness*. Unfortunately, unforgiveness in our heart does not autocorrect; it requires an apology and a change of heart. Love does not keep a count of wrongdoings but does ask to be forgiven. Have you lost a friendship because you failed to ask for forgiveness? Could there be fault on both sides, and even if there is not, could you forgive as God has forgiven you? Forgiveness does not always grant access back into your life, but it gives God room to heal the wound.

♻ **Share:** Transparency is an important part of being a Christ follower. We are not perfect, just forgiven. We are in the process of sanctification—a big word for the process of being disciplined and discipled into the character of Christ. My (Kathy's) friend T. W. S. Hunt would say that the process is not complete until God "graduates" us to heaven. Those who feel ashamed and unworthy need to know that we all need forgiveness. Share your testimony honestly with someone today.

Love Prefers Others above Ourselves

Do nothing from selfish ambition or conceit, but in humility count others more significant than yourselves. Let each of you look not only to his own interests, but also to the interests of others. Have this mind among yourselves, which is yours in Christ Jesus.

Philippians 2:3–5

EXPERIENCE GOD'S LOVE

How many times is selfish ambition and pride mixed in with our motives to be used by God? The Bible speaks of a time when our true motives will be revealed (1 Corinthians 4:5). How do we come to a place where our labor in the kingdom of God is truly pure? How do we come to a place where, deep in our hearts, our only desire is for God to receive the glory He deserves?

Sometimes it can be difficult to get a handle on what love should look like in everyday life. Having an intellectual understanding that to love someone means to prefer them above ourselves is an excellent starting point. Knowing that love means to prefer others above ourselves is a clear target to aim at in every circumstance.

Then allow God's Spirit to work this preference of others deep into your heart. A willingness to prefer others above ourselves can only come from Him. We all naturally prefer ourselves above others. Therefore, this new life in the Spirit is completely counter-intuitive to our human nature. Yet at the same time, this sacrificial love is the very nature of God's Spirit, and He lives inside of us.

If we are struggling to live out a life of preferring others above ourselves, it can only mean that we are holding on to our lives again. God's Spirit never struggles with laying His life down for the betterment of others. If He is truly in control, then we will see this same willingness to die to ourselves flowing supernaturally in and through us.

Another step to this selfless love becoming our daily reality, is to learn to care about the interests of others. We can become so preoccupied with our own concerns that we don't even take the time to be aware of the needs of others. If that is you, slow down and learn to ask questions such as, "What is something you are facing right now that I could pray for?" As you learn to be attentive to the needs of those around you, you can expect a supernatural increase in your willingness to care for others. This selfless love is the hallmark of a mature, Christlike disciple.

Father, I acknowledge that preferring others above myself does not come naturally to me. In fact, it is impossible apart from your assistance. Yet, I believe it is your will for me at all times. Therefore, I ask you to work this preference of others in me and through me for your glory. I thank you for this Christlike love in advance, and I look forward to the lives that you will choose to impact through me.

EXPRESS GOD'S LOVE

When was the last time you set aside your plans or preferences to do what someone else wanted to do, or even to do something the way they wanted it done? Do you find it easier to consider, and even sacrifice, to meet the interests or needs of others, than it is to surrender to doing things their way? It's okay to smile or giggle, you are probably thinking of your own example right now. Love is reflected in the desire to humble ourselves and serve others; it seeks to delight their heart and not just get the job done or the mission accomplished.

Prayer: Lord, thank you for always knowing what I need physically, emotionally, mentally, and especially spiritually. Jesus, thank you for putting aside all the comforts of heaven to come down to earth in flesh to show and tell us all about your love. You chose to surrender your life on a cruel cross. You could have called down thousands of angels from heaven to defend you, but you suffered excruciating pain and the wrath of the Father to take away my sin. Open my eyes to the ways that I can put others before myself but never put anyone before you.

Care: There are opportunities every day to pause and be considerate of others. These can be small, such as allowing someone to check out in front of you, holding the door open for someone, or paying for the meal or coffee of the person behind you. There are also big ways: long days helping someone move, long-term commitments to plan and implement a project, or longer journeys that offer consistent help on an ongoing basis. Few people have room in their schedule to add another thing, but you can always make room in your heart for people. Let your heart rearrange your schedule.

♻ **Share:** You have probably heard, "It is more blessed to give than to receive" (Acts 20:35). There is a joy in giving, happiness in helping, and delight in doing for others. We do for others because it shows our love for God as we show love for others. There is no greater joy than watching someone receive Jesus as their Lord and Savior—that's the only time when there is no greater blessing than to receive. Share Christ's message courageously and pray that many will receive.

Let's Get Real

Jesus looked at them and said, "With man this is impossible, but with God all things are possible."

Matthew 19:26

EXPERIENCE GOD'S LOVE

A man looked out his window one morning and decided he was going to fly. He had seen the birds do it. Why not him? Having mustered up his courage, he walked to a nearby hill and climbed to the top. Looking out over the surrounding countryside, he proceeded to run with all his might and then jump as high and as far as he could while simultaneously flapping his arms. His flight lasted all of two seconds. What lasted longer was the extended tumble down half of the hill, complete with bruises and scrapes up his back and down both arms.

Have you ever attempted with the best of your abilities to unconditionally love those around you? How did that go for you? Perhaps you have had the same experiences I (Chris) have had. Many times I have committed myself to really love those around me. I mustered up all my strength and went out with new resolve, only to fail multiple times by the middle of that same day.

God's kind of love is not *humanly* possible. How many of us, if we honestly examine our thoughts, speech, and actions, are loving our spouses and family members the way God intends us to? How about our roommates, employers, classmates, or neighbors? Who is living out a lifestyle of consistent, persistent self-sacrificial love that turns the other cheek, goes the extra mile, and never asks for anything in return?

We can know that God desires us to live in a certain way. We can give it lip service and even dabble in it, but when we purposefully seek to live out our lives in the way the Word of God instructs us to, that is when we realize that God's ways are not our ways. The truth is, He is not expecting us to muster up the necessary love to change the world. He is really calling us to come to Him so that His Spirit can live out what we never could.

Let's discard the fake for His reality. Let's be real and acknowledge where we really are in this whole loving-like-God thing. The sooner we humble ourselves and confess how woefully lacking in Godlike love we are, the sooner God will show us the path of grace that can lead us to embrace His unfathomable love for us. Then, from that place of His embrace, we can trust God to love the world through us.

Father, I thank you that you are not expecting me to attempt to love others in my own efforts. I acknowledge that your type of love is humanly impossible. Teach me how to trust you to love others through me. I know it is possible through you, therefore I expectantly trust you to teach me how to allow your love to flow in and through me.

EXPRESS GOD'S LOVE

You have probably heard it said, "God enables those whom He calls," or "Where God guides, He provides." Whether you feel these are catchy or corny phrases, they are truth. God does not command or call us to do anything that He does not have His heart and hands in; with Him *all* He desires and requires is possible. God calls us to love, and He equips and enables us to love. Is there something you know you are supposed to do, but you think it is too difficult or will take too much effort? Start walking and working in faith as you ask God to guide and provide for His glory.

👤 **Prayer:** Lord, thank you for your love and patience. I desire to fulfill every purpose and plan you have authored for my life. Thank you for allowing imperfect people to be a part of your kingdom; thank you for calling us to share your love and message. I know with you, God, all things are possible. Help me to love those who dislike or push me away. Equip me to love in your strength and Spirit.

❤️ **Care:** One of the best ways to let someone know that you care about them is to show it before you say it. Let your actions do the talking, and if necessary, the convincing. The church cannot claim to be about love if we are not out and about showing love. Where do you know there is a need that you could help fill? Think and pray about someone who has been "impossible" to love; ask God to show you a need or interest in their life where you can connect and care.

⚠ **Share:** Many times Christians choose not to share the message of Jesus with the people they love the most because they do not want the relationship to get awkward or cause them to pull away. Sadly, they are willing to lose them for eternity and watch them miss a lifetime of blessings just to keep things comfortable between them. Share your faith in casual conversations, and ask faith questions and be willing to listen without interrupting. Find connection points and be willing to say, "I don't know, let's look for that answer together" when they ask questions you do not know about. Never guess or make up an answer—being a disciple means being a lifelong student of Jesus.

Section Two

MEDITATING ON GOD'S GREAT LOVE

Finally, brothers, whatever is true, whatever is honorable, whatever is just, whatever is pure, whatever is lovely, whatever is commendable, if there is any excellence, if there is anything worthy of praise, think about these things.

Philippians 4:8

We want to become a people of love. But how do we do it? What if we took time to meditate on God's love? How would this begin to change our lives?

Have you ever heard the expression, "You are what you eat"? This refers to the fact that if you eat healthy food, your body will become stronger, and if you eat an unhealthy diet, your body will suffer the consequences. There is certainly some truth to this as it relates to our physical bodies. In a similar way, Paul is encouraging us to eat good spiritual food, believing that this will lead to a healthy spiritual life.

We want to take the next nine days to dive deeply into God's love. To meditate on it. To allow for our misperceptions about love to be exposed and removed. To reflect on the ramifications of God's love and how it is supposed to impact all facets of our lives.

Father, I thank you for this unique opportunity to meditate on your great love. I ask that you penetrate deeply into my heart, revealing to me the ways that I have not really known your love for me. Transform me from within so that I can carry your love to others.

God Loves You Unconditionally

God shows his love for us in that while we were still sinners, Christ died for us.

Romans 5:8

EXPERIENCE GOD'S LOVE

Many times, we can get into a rut with God where we think that we must perform to earn His love. The truth is, we have all been indoctrinated in some form of conditional love. That is the only kind of love that fleshly humanity understands—a love that gives as long as we are receiving something of equal or greater value in return. At home, at school, at work, and beyond, most of our life experiences have ingrained in us an understanding that if we perform well, we will be appreciated and cared for. And if we fail, we have come to accept shame, disapproval, and in some cases, even hatred, as the norm.

To break out of this conditional love mentality, it will take a revelation from God. Only the Spirit of God can reveal to our hearts just how much He is for us and not against us. He has given us His Word to break through a faulty understanding of His love. In this passage in Romans, we learn that even while we were God's enemies, He loved us enough to die for us! Jesus said there is no greater love than to be willing to lay down our lives for another person. So, the truth is, God loved you at the greatest measure possible while you were still living in complete rebellion against Him.

If He loved you with the greatest act of love when you hated Him, can you believe that He loves you today? May the Spirit of God have mercy on all of us, so that we will once and for all break free from the lies that would have us believe that God's love is conditional.

He loves you. He will never stop loving you. His love is what you need. Will you allow His unconditional love to embrace you now?

Father, I desire to understand your love for me. I give you my sin, my shame, and the feelings of condemnation that I have wrestled with. I choose to embrace the truth of your Word and believe that you love me simply for who I am and not based on my performance. I thank you that your love for me is the same yesterday, today, and forever.

EXPRESS GOD'S LOVE

Before I confessed my sin and my need for a Savior, Christ died for me. Before I was convicted of my sinful life, Christ offered forgiveness. Christ's invitation for abundant life came while I was living abandoned. Before we took our first breaths, Christ took His last on the cross, bearing the sin and shame that would separate us from the Father. He willingly became the bridge to forgiveness and faith before your birth. What do you say to a Savior who loved you and suffered for you before you loved Him? In understanding this truth for yourself, you must embrace this truth for every person; while they are yet sinners, Christ died for them, and He wants you to love them as He loved you.

Prayer: Lord, thank you for dying for me, for offering me abundant and eternal life. Forgive me for my judgmental thoughts toward others. You alone are the judge, and I am called to be a messenger of your love. Show me how to love those who are living in opposition to your ways. Strengthen me to share your love with those who do not love you yet.

Care: Can you think of someone that you have a hard time imagining Christ loving? Is it someone who practices a different religion or lifestyle? Is there someone whom you can think of in your workplace, neighborhood, or school that seems far from God but that God has put near to you? Ask God how you can show care for them. Begin by being friendly and then make honest, pure-hearted attempts to get to know them and something about their family, history, or life. Find commonalities to have conversations about. Allow them to get to know what it means to not be rejected by a Christ follower, so that they might someday be open to accepting Christ.

☁ Share: "Just as I Am" is a famous hymn that professes that when we come to Jesus, we have nothing to confess but that His blood was shed for us. We can never "clean ourselves up" or do enough good to present ourselves favorably before Holy God. We should never expect a disciple's behavior from an un-discipled person. Share Christ's love before a lesson or lecture about Christlike behavior. Jesus changes hearts and then He changes behavior.

We Are God's Children

See what kind of love the Father has given to us, that we should be called children of God; and so we are.

1 John 3:1

EXPERIENCE GOD'S LOVE

God's children. Have you ever stopped long enough for this truth to really sink in? You are God's child. You are His son or His daughter. You stand on this earth as a child of the King of Glory. You are an earthly representation of the family of God. Your heavenly Daddy is the rightful owner of all things. He is in full control of every detail of human history—past, present, and future.

Nothing can happen to you unless it first passes through the sovereign hands of your eternal Father. You have nothing to fear. There is nothing that you will ever need to worry about. Ever. Under any circumstances.

Allow your heavenly Father to embrace you in this moment. Allow the truth of His sovereignty and His affectionate parental love for you to so infuse you with divine courage that you will never be the same again.

No matter what your earthly family may have been like, you

now have a heavenly family, made up of sisters and brothers from all over the world. You now have a Father who is interested in the uniqueness of you. He cares so very much about you. He loves the special things that make you who you are. He delights in you. He wants to listen to you. He wants to hear about what you are facing. He will never leave you or forsake you. Not now. Not ever. On into eternity, He will still be there caring for you.

Entrust yourself to Him today. Allow His fatherly Spirit to father you. Allow Him to speak into your life. He has nothing but your best interests at heart. When He speaks to you about anything, listen well and seek to apply His instructions in your daily practice. In this way, He will become far more than a distant spiritual Father, but your moment-by-moment best friend and confidant. Your leader and the lover of your soul.

Heavenly Father, I need you to father me. Deep in my heart, I want to know that you are my Father and that I am your beloved child. Help me to rest in your love for me. Teach me what it means to live close to you so that I fulfill the reason why you have adopted me into your family.

EXPRESS GOD'S LOVE

As you proceed through the 40 Days of Love, continue to look for ways to express the love of Jesus in the moment, throughout the day, in projects that can be done in a day, and in longer commitments of thought and time. Love is part of a Jesus follower's lifestyle that should be expressed personally and also exhibited with others from various neighborhoods, churches, schools, and workplaces, throughout your community. Many hands make work light and a delight; pray and proceed with a project that brings people together. Meet needs and meet your neighbors.

👤 **Prayer:** Lord, I am deeply grateful to know that I am your child. Let my heart and hands speak and serve in ways that show you are my Father. Help me to personally and corporately take your Word and love to my neighborhood and city. Let me be a spark that ignites many hearts to share love in your name. I continue to bring you the people I have written down on my Prayer-Care-Share lists. Let my heart burn and my mind search for ways to share your love as you reveal yourself to them, that they may be children of God.

♥ **Care:** Love begins in your family. It is important for your family to know your commitment to the 40 Days of Love. Invite them to join you on the journey. Even young children can write or tell you the names of people they want on their own Prayer-Care-Share list. Encourage them to invite friends to church or special events or to share their faith in schoolwork or in clubs and activities. Invite neighbors to your home for meals or family game nights, and include the whole family in showing care for others.

⚠ **Share:** Love begins at home, in your house and neighborhood. God planted you in the midst of people who need to hear His Word, who need to be told the good news of Jesus and how to know Jesus as Lord and Savior. There are many great sharing resources, including "Engagers" from everyhomeusa.com, DVDs, apps, and video clips in fourteen hundred languages from the Jesusfilm.org, the "Four Spiritual Laws" from crustore.org, and many others. It is vital that you do not just stuff resources in a front door, but that you meet people face-to-face and talk with them as you put these resources in their hands. You can do this! Go and make disciples.

True Love Disciplines

> *My son, do not despise the Lord's discipline or be weary of his reproof, for the Lord reproves him whom he loves, as a father the son in whom he delights.*

Proverbs 3:11–12

EXPERIENCE GOD'S LOVE

Following a firm punishment, my (Chris') friend's son said to him, "I know you tell me that you love me when you discipline me, but it doesn't feel like love." My friend asked him, "What does love feel like?" His son said, "Love feels good."

My friend then replied, "That is only one side to love. There's another side to love, and that is a love that hurts." He then shared the following illustration: "There was a blind man who was going to walk off a cliff. In order to attempt to save him, you ran and tackled him, but in the process you broke his arm. At first, the man was angry because you hurt him. But once he realized that he was on the edge of a cliff, he actually became grateful for his broken arm and thanked you for saving him from something much worse."

Our modern understanding of love often rules out any form of discipline as being compatible with genuine care and concern. In contrast to our cultural understanding of love, the Word of

God shows a different kind of love—a love that understands that there are times when discipline is the most caring response to sinful behavior.

Even a peripheral examination of the Bible shows us that discipline, sometimes in forms that we would view as extreme, is all part of true love. True love does not mean that we tolerate sin. True love does not just look the other way when someone is in slavery to sin. God's type of love cares enough about people to compel them to forsake their sin.

From encouraging spankings, to showing that trials lead to positive change, God's Word shows us that He allows difficulties to come into the lives of those He loves. This is not to say that every difficulty we face is God punishing us. It is to say that God does not blush at punishment the way that we may. He understands that it is a necessary part of life, and His motive is that we will become all that He intended for us. He loves us too much to allow us to stay the way we are, if where we are is not in the likeness of His Son, Jesus.

Instead of running from the discipline of the Lord, let us humble ourselves and allow God's Spirit to use it to mold us more and more into His image.

Father, I choose to thank you for your discipline. I believe that you love me at all times, and therefore I believe that even your discipline is an expression of your love for me. Help me to humble myself and allow your discipline to work in me the Christlike life that you desire. Thank you for working all things together for my good.

EXPRESS GOD'S LOVE

Have you ever encountered a child who was left to do as they pleased as their parents ignored their inappropriate and even disruptive behavior? How does that reflect on the heart of the parent? What will the future look like for a child who knows no boundaries or consequences? Discipline is dispensed from the heart with love. It is not a force that lashes out in anger and frustration, but it guides behavior and provides consequences. Discipline builds a strong foundation of character and maturity and will provide favor and opportunity throughout life. Discipline helps avoid detours from your destiny.

👤 **Prayer:** Lord, as your child I receive your discipline, knowing it comes through your heart for my best blessings today and for my future. Search me and show me anything that is unpleasing to you in my life. Correct me so that my life draws others to you. I do not want to disgrace you with a life of pride or hurtful behavior. I do not want to be labeled a hypocrite, but rather a pure heart that loves you and others deeply and honestly.

♥ **Care:** People in prison are being disciplined for breaking the law; they made terrible choices for a variety of reasons, and their lives have roots that run deep with the need for forgiveness and a chance to walk in the light and life that God planned for them. Unfortunately, many are forever marked with their crime, and those who get a second chance at life outside prison often return to crime because they do not have the skills or opportunities to provide for themselves or their families. Pray for prisoners and their families. Pray about getting involved with local and national ministries that minister to the families of prisoners as well as those in prison.

♻ **Share:** We are all sinners who need a Savior. We have all made mistakes, sinned, and suffered discipline and consequences. Grace and mercy washes away shame but the lessons remain. Be willing to share that your life is not perfect, that you have regrets. God disciplines us, teaches us, forgives us, and enables us to turn away from sin and get back on His path for our lives. Be willing to be transparent and share an experience where God disciplined you and how you responded to Him.

God's Holiness Compels Us to Love

"Holy, holy, holy, is the Lord God Almighty, who was and is and is to come!"

Revelation 4:8

EXPERIENCE GOD'S LOVE

This is the song that the angels are singing to God forever and ever. As followers of Christ it is vitally important for us to understand the marriage of love and holiness. The same being who is perfect love is also perfectly holy.

The apostle John tells us that, "Whoever says 'I know him' but does not keep his commandments is a liar, and the truth is not in him" (1 John 2:4). Proverbs tells us, "The fear of the LORD IS THE BEGINNING OF WISDOM" (Proverbs 9:10). Jesus told us, "I will warn you whom to fear: fear him who, after he has killed, has authority to cast into hell. Yes, I tell you, fear him!" (Luke 12:5).

What does it mean to properly fear God? How is fear compatible with love?

Jesus on the cross is the perfect visual merging of God's love and God's holiness. We see God's hatred of sin and the just punishment for our rebellion against Him. Simultaneously, we see

God's perfect love for us, as He was willing to suffer on our behalf so that we could be forgiven.

The reverential fear that we are called to walk in does not invalidate the love of God. In fact, a proper fear of God leads to a deeper understanding of biblical love. When we realize that biblical love for God is more than having a happy feeling, but choosing to prefer Him above ourselves, we can see the great value of having a revelation of God's holiness.

We need to see His holiness. Only as we see Him in His holiness will we consistently choose His will above our own selfish inclinations. The reality is that we often need more than a happy feeling in order to choose God's ways. We often need an awareness that if we choose to go with our selfish desires, we are rebelling against a Holy God, and there will be consequences.

When we have a revelation of the holiness of God, this causes us to see our need to submit to God in every area of our lives. His holiness compels us to turn away from compromise. In this way, God's love and God's holiness are perfectly compatible. His holiness leads us to a biblical love for God and others. A proper fear of the Lord compels us to love and worship God not just with our lips but with the whole of our lives.

Father, I ask for your forgiveness for the times that I have neglected a proper reverential fear of you. Today I ask that you would reveal to me what it means to live with a deep awareness of your holiness, and at the same time live with a deep awareness of your love for me. Your holiness and your love are perfectly compatible. Help me to model your holiness and your love.

EXPRESS GOD'S LOVE

God's holiness is just one of the attributes that makes it impossible for Him to disregard our sinfulness. Our sinfulness could never dwell in the presence of His holiness; we were separated from God until Jesus came to pay our sin debt in full. Jesus felt the full wrath of God for all our sins on the cross. He offered his blood to wash away our sin so that He could usher us into the holy presence of our Father in heaven. He is most holy, separate, and sacred—the one true God.

Prayer: Lord, you are holy, holy, holy! You are high and lifted up; you have always been and always will be. You are King of Kings and the Lord of my heart and life. Mold my life with your hands and love so that I am your vessel, sacred and useful for your purposes. I want my life to be lived in holy reverence as you reveal your supremacy in my life and across the universe.

Care: We are called to be holy, consecrated, and separated from the filth of this world and our flesh, to be in this world but not of it. Abiding in His love and lordship with the Holy Spirit living inside us is what sets us apart. We rise above the gossip, cussing, or selfishness around us and do unto others as we would have them do to us. Christ's holiness enables us to be holy in his hands and to do things we never dreamed possible or would have ever done in our own flesh. Is there someone at work, school, or even church that is left out, teased, or bullied? Show them kindness today—stand up for them or invite them to sit with you or go to lunch. Do more than just refuse to be part of the abuse; be part of the healing.

♻ **Share:** You may have spent most of your life trying not to stand out, but God calls us to be set apart. This does not make us egotistical. God's holiness brings healing and forgiveness so that we can only boast in Him. Holy people are humble people; share your testimony of how Christ's sacrifice saved you. Share how His blood alone can restore a right relationship with Holy God.

God Desires All People to Be Saved

God our Savior ... desires all people to be saved and to come to the knowledge of the truth.

1 Timothy 2:3–4

EXPERIENCE GOD'S LOVE

God desires. That in and of itself is an amazing reality. The God who created the universe has desires that have not been fully realized. His heart longs to see everyone saved from their sin and walking in His truth.

Jesus talks about His search for lost souls being like a loving father who has an estranged son. When his rebellious son returns to him, he runs to him, puts the best robe on him, and puts a ring on his hand and sandals on his feet. Then he asks for the fattened calf to be killed and a great celebration to take place: "My son was dead, and is alive again; he was lost, and is found," shouts the heart of our heavenly Father (Luke 15:24).

Is this how you view God? Do you see Him as a being who is so in love with His creation that He would do anything to win us back? Do you realize that He is willing to climb any mountain, cross any sea, and pay any price so that we will see the value of living in relationship with Him?

So many who claim Christ do not know God's heart for them, and therefore they do not understand the Father's heart for those who are opposed to the gospel. God haters are loved by the one they hate. God loves atheists, agnostics, devil worshipers, sorcerers, prostitutes, drug dealers, and murderers. We may not understand it, but no one has so sinned against Him that God does not still love them. Remember that we serve the King who left His throne to live among sinners so that He might restore our relationship with Him.

This searching, longing, desirous heart of love for His creation cannot be underestimated and cannot be overstated. God was willing to die so that mankind could know Him. If He was willing to do that for you, what else would He not be willing to do to see everyone you know come to Jesus? The most radical evangelism that we have ever heard of is nothing compared to what He has already done to ensure that our souls are saved.

Do we have His zealous heart of love beating inside of us for the hurting and the broken? Do we long for opportunities to share our faith in Jesus with those who do not yet know Him? If not, we would be wise to sit at the feet of Jesus and ask Him to impart to us His desire for everyone to be saved.

Father, I acknowledge that I have not completely understood your heart for those who do not know you. In this moment, I ask that you fill me with your heart's desire for lost souls. Empower me to be your hands and feet and voice to every life that you have placed around me.

EXPRESS GOD'S LOVE

Imagine the celebration in heaven every time a heart says yes to Jesus and a soul is secured. Imagine the Father's joy as the wages of sin are stamped "Paid in full" and wrath is washed away with grace and mercy. How does your heart celebrate when someone professes faith in Jesus? What part can you play today in planting a seed of love, watering faith, or nurturing knowledge so that Jesus' love is known and grown in another soul that God desires to be saved?

Prayer: Lord, thank you that I get to join in on the heavenly "Hallelujahs" as people turn from certain death to abundant life. Give me your heart for ALL to be saved, to know you, and to live out their lives in the shadow of your supremacy. Let them be filled with your love and lessons as your disciples.

Care: As catastrophic weather moves across the world, people suffer loss and destruction in personal and profound ways. Political unrest around the world sends victims running for their lives with only the clothes on their backs. Epidemics of disease, fires, and terrorism leave us speechless and heartbroken. What evil uses to destroy can be opportunities to show kingdom love and compassion to those next door or around the world. Ministries that respond with help and hope in these circumstances are known as compassion ministries. Would you consider going through certified training to respond to disasters? Have you ever given blood, time, talent, or treasure? Would you go help clean up and rebuild after a disaster, or help refugees learn

English or a skill, or provide transportation for school and services? How would you want people to respond if you lost everything? Do unto others …

⬥ **Share:** The last thing that people need in times of loss and destruction is someone pounding a Bible and yelling about the wrath and judgment of God. Hate and judgment never open doors or hearts. We live in a broken world; sin scarred all of creation. Nature groans for Christ's return and its restoration to the beginning statement of "it was good." In times of trouble, leave the convicting up to the Holy Spirit and focus on loving people to Christ, not pushing them away. Share hope and love as you help to restore some normal pace and place for life.

Without Love We Can Accomplish Nothing

If I have prophetic powers, and understand all mysteries and all knowledge, and if I have all faith, so as to remove mountains, but have not love, I am nothing. If I give away all I have, and if I deliver up my body to be burned, but have not love, I gain nothing.

1 Corinthians 13:2–3

EXPERIENCE GOD'S LOVE

Paul makes it clear here that it is possible to experience the power of God moving in and through our lives yet fail to have love. Many people run here and there seeking spectacular evidence of God's power in their lives. This is not new. Jesus said to the Pharisees, "An evil and adulterous generation seeks for a sign, but no sign will be given to it except the sign of the prophet Jonah" (Matthew 12:39). Paul cautioned that even if we possess the power to understand all knowledge, and have faith that moves mountains, without love, we are nothing. Amazingly, he continued by stating that if we are willing to give up all that we own and be brutally killed, but are without love, we "gain nothing."

Let this truth sink in. Paul, a man who healed the sick, raised the dead (Acts 20:10), planted churches among the unreached, and who endured beatings for his faith, declared that all of it is nothing if we fail to love. Elsewhere, Paul stated the value of prophesy, healings, faith, and the surrender of our material possessions for the purpose of advancing Christ's kingdom.[4] So he is not saying spiritual power is without value; he is simply putting it into perspective. Love is paramount.

Is God's Spirit calling you to simplify your spiritual quest? Have you found yourself pursuing the power of God but lacking His love? What if instead, you simply began to pursue a wholehearted love of God that would position you to deeply love all those He brings into your life? Could it be that this approach to your spiritual growth would result in more lasting fruit? Allow the Spirit of God to put love in its proper place, so that everything you do is done out of love.

Father, I ask for your forgiveness for times when I have sought to represent you without a deep and real expression of your love. Today, I choose to believe that love is the most important thing. I choose to pursue your love for me and for others above all things.

---

4   See 1 Corinthians 12:7–11 and 2 Corinthians 9:6–7.

EXPRESS GOD'S LOVE

Have you ever known someone who was very smart and influential but you really did not enjoy being around them? Sadly, pride or arrogance can often, but not always, follow the gift of knowledge and power that God intended to be clothed in love. We must recognize that every opportunity, position, possession, and prestige is from God, for His purposes and glory. You are blessed to be a blessing; you are given gifts to share them, not store them. We steward our resources and relationships so that others do not have to scrounge for theirs. The key to all of this is love—love that seeks satisfaction in quiet, humble ways to bring joy to others.

Prayer: Lord, all that I have is yours; all that I am is because of you. Let all that you give to me flow through my life like living water, in and out of my hands and heart. I want to speak and serve with love. I want my faith and your kingdom to grow in love. Pull out any root of pride or weed of selfishness in my life so that I may show and share your love and message.

Care: Where do you have influence that could help another person at work or in your area of interest and influence? Who can you quietly give a hand up and not just a handout? Let love lead you to mentor, champion an opportunity, or speak up on someone's behalf to give them a chance or even a second chance.

Share: Studies of the brain show that the subconscious of every human is first concerned with preservation and safety. The brain is always asking, "Am I safe?" If the answer is yes, then the brain asks, "Am I cared for?" Only after these two questions are answered positively is the brain able to ask, "What can I learn?"[5] Think about that for a moment. People who fear for their lives, or don't have food or shelter, do not have the capacity to listen, learn, and receive the message of Jesus. It is not that they are rejecting Jesus; it is that they are not capable of even conceiving and receiving. How does this change the way you think and share faith from this day forward? Always lead with love and care before you share.

---

5   https://thejournal.com/articles/2014/06/02/teaching-the-brain-to-learn.aspx

Day 17

Love Is Always a Choice

Let all that you do be done in love.

1 Corinthians 16:14

EXPERIENCE GOD'S LOVE

Imagine taking a single day and purposing to prefer others above yourself in every single decision. Every thought, every spoken word, and every action. From the moment you wake up to the time you go to bed. A day of loving others more than you love yourself.

What kind of impact do you think that day would have in eternity? How many lives would you have the opportunity to touch in a single day? Now imagine this "love day" is extended into a week. How many more lives would God use you to bless? Now, how about a month of love that leads you into a sustained lifestyle? You would probably be a completely different person by the end of that time. God would have so shifted your attitude that all you would care about is the needs of others.

In a way, that is the purpose of this book and the heart of this Scripture. God's Word is speaking of a life where the totality of who we are and what we do is done in love at all times. This is what we have been created for. To care so deeply for others that every second of our lives is expended for God's glory and the betterment of others. This is what it means to be true children of God, modeling the same type of love that compelled Him to die for our sins.

This life of love at all times and in every circumstance is a life of impact. It is a life of continuously storing up treasures in heaven. It is a life of no regrets, because we are living every moment for His glory. Let's take up this verse not merely as a challenge but as a promise from God. He would not ask us to do something that is not possible through His Spirit. God is promising us that a life of love is possible at all times.

Father, I thank you that you love me completely at all times. I thank you that you model for me what it means to love in everything you do. I believe this Word is a promise to me that it is possible to live in love at all times. I ask you to show me how to walk in love no matter what I am facing, and I thank you for it in advance.

EXPRESS GOD'S LOVE

The apostle Paul tells the people in Corinth, "Be on the alert, stand firm in the faith, act like men, be strong. Let all that you do be done in love" (1 Corinthians 16:13–14). In doing all that you do in love, you can tie these points together. Love keeps a lookout: it is alert for friend and foe. Love stands firm: it is not wishy-washy or a fair-weather feeling. Love is mature, not based on your mood, and love is a choice that we make in every attitude, affection, and action.

Prayer: Lord, my whole life is yours. I will not divide it out as secular and spiritual or mine and yours; it all belongs to you. I commit to doing everything in love—your love. In your power and in your will, I know that every conversation, every decision, every meeting, every moment of my day can be walked out and worked out in love.

Care: Do you ever think of Sunday as "the Lord's day" and Monday as a workday? The truth is, they are all God's days. Your life in the workplace serves Jesus just as your time at church does. God gifted you to do what you do, whether you are an accountant, a CEO, a custodian, serve in the military, or take care of your home and children. What you do brings Him glory and serves His purposes in the kingdom picture. Pastors and faith-based organization leaders are not the only people in "full-time ministry;" all Christ followers are in full-time ministry. Everything you do and the way you do it matters to God. Prepare to care as you drive to work each day.

♻ **Share:** Love is a calling and a command, a tone and a touch, and it is minimized or magnified in all that we do. You can take out the trash or clean the bathroom with a cheerful heart because you are happy to have the provisions to have garbage and a home with a bathroom. Make a choice to share love with people throughout your day. Check your posture, your expressions, the timing of your responses, as well as the cheerfulness and gratefulness that you express to others all day. If someone asks, "Why are you in such a good mood?" or "Why would you do that for me?" share what Jesus has lovingly done for you. Share His love.

A Finished Work

A person is not justified by works of the law but through faith in Jesus Christ ...

Galatians 2:16

EXPERIENCE GOD'S LOVE

The gospel is amazingly good news. What Jesus Christ has accomplished through His sacrifice on the cross is totally sufficient. He has already fulfilled the righteous demands of the law of God. Do you believe this? Do you walk in this good news as your daily inheritance?

Sadly, many of us fall into a great falsehood, thinking that our salvation is somehow based on the work of Jesus plus our obedience to the law. Even many sincere followers of Christ slowly lose sight of just how good the good news is meant to be.

Paul makes a very plain statement: "A person is not justified by works of the law but through faith in Jesus Christ." He goes on to say, "By works of the law no one will be justified" (Galatians 2:16). Faith in Christ alone is what produces salvation. None of our obedience to the law can ever save our souls.

Many of us seem to have a hard time really believing this truth. Perhaps we still want to take partial credit for our salvation.

We may hold on to some shred of hope that there is something good in us apart from Christ's grace. Perhaps other Scriptures have confused us when they state, "Faith apart from works is dead" (James 2:26). Instead of understanding that true biblical faith in Christ produces lifestyle transformation, we can start to believe that the level of lifestyle transformation we have experienced is what determines our salvation.

Lifestyle transformation is biblical and critical if the good news is to be attractive. At the same time, may we never claim that our justification in the eyes of God has anything to do with our level of obedience to the law.

Praise God that the gospel is based solely on what Jesus accomplished. It is a free gift of God. What Jesus did through His perfect life, death, and resurrection is a finished work. We enter into the reality of His finished work by faith alone, through grace alone.

Jesus, I thank you that you have already paid the penalty for all my sins. I believe through your death and resurrection that I have been made right with God based solely on what you have done for me and not because of anything that I have done or will ever do. Teach me to rest in your finished work.

EXPRESS GOD'S LOVE

Jesus fulfilled the law, and now the Spirit fills us so that we are able to do all that God has planned for us. We are not saved by obeying the law, but we express love by obeying God. Our response to the gift of salvation is to love Him and love people, all people. In expressing love, you grow as a disciple and store up treasures in heaven. Christ's work on the cross expressed the deepest, most sacrificial love of all. Let that love continue to live out in your Prayer-Care-Share lifestyle.

Prayer: Lord, thank you for your finished work on the cross. Your blood covers my sin. You were the only one who could perfectly keep the law, and so you finished the work of the law and ushered in grace. Help me to express to others that my life is a work in progress; I am not perfect, but I am being perfected by you and in you.

Care: One of the greatest ways to care for someone is to invite them to your church. There are many learning opportunities such as Sunday morning service, Sunday school, small groups, Bible studies, and more. There are great fellowships and activities, opportunities to serve the community, concerts or movie premiers, youth gatherings, Vacation Bible School, the list goes on and on. People need fellowship. We were not made for isolation, especially spiritual isolation. Make it a habit to invite people to church, and make sure that visitors not only feel welcomed that day but are convinced by love to stay.

⛰ **Share:** Many people who have never experienced the love of Jesus think of church and Christianity as a club filled with rules and unreachable expectations. The church is the body of Christ, made up of every person who lives their life under the love and lordship of Jesus in faith that He is the perfect, risen, living Son of God. His commands protect us; they do not steal our fun but rather add to our joy. There is safety and protection, peace and comfort under the wings of God's authority. In the finished work of the cross, we can enter into the presence of God with praise and thanksgiving. Christianity is about a relationship with Jesus, not a building full of rules.

Day 19

Love Is
the Greatest Thing

"Teacher, which is the great commandment in the Law?"
And he said to him, "You shall love the Lord your God with
all your heart and with all your soul and with all your mind.
This is the great and first commandment. And a second is
like it: You shall love your neighbor as yourself. On these two
commandments depend all the Law and the Prophets."

Matthew 22:36–40

EXPERIENCE GOD'S LOVE

Mount Everest is known as the earth's highest mountain. With
an elevation of over 29,000 feet, it has no other competition. The
thought of climbing to the summit has captivated the imagi-
nation of mountaineers for decades. It was not until 1953 that
Edmund Hillary and Tenzing Norgay made the first official
ascent.[6] Previously many had died trying.

In this passage in Matthew, Jesus presents us with a spiritual
Mount Everest. This summit stands head and shoulders above
any other spiritual pursuit we may have had. The Pharisees were

---

6   *Wikipedia*, s.v. "Mount Everest," https://en.wikipedia.org/w/index.php?title=Mount
    _Everest&oldid=773583690 (accessed April 9, 2017).

gathered together, and one of them asked Him what the greatest commandment was. Unflinching, Jesus stated that it is to love God and to love others with all that we have. Everything else hangs on these two things.

Happily for us, we do not need to attempt to climb this spiritual mountain in our own strength. If that were the case, none of us would be able to reach the summit. The key is to realize that Jesus already lives at the top of this mountain. He is not inviting us to try to climb up through our own efforts. He is inviting us to die to ourselves so that He can live His life of love through us.

There are many earthly and spiritual pursuits that we could choose to go after. Jesus narrows the playing field here. He effectively says, "Pursue me for this, and I will take care of all the rest." Simultaneously, He lets us know that if we miss this, we've missed it all.

As followers of Christ, love for God and love for others is the summit we should have our eyes fixed on. As we surrender our lives completely to Jesus, we can expect His Holy Spirit to live a life of sacrificial love in and through us.

Father, I thank you for making it clear to me that love for you and love for others is the most important thing. I thank you that I do not have to attempt to live out this lifestyle on my own. Today I ask you to live your life of love in and through me for your glory.

EXPRESS GOD'S LOVE

While recently visiting another country, I (Kathy) resolved to watch for ways that we were alike instead of focusing on the differences. I chose to look for similarities they shared with me, Americans, and Christians, even though the people who lived there were very diverse. It was fun to watch parents care for their children and husbands hug their wives. People hurried to work, waved and called out to friends; the likenesses were abundant. I even met a girl who could have been mistaken for the twin of a dear friend, right down to her converse sneakers. There is a lot to be said for our likenesses. Look for them as connection points to share and show the love and message of Jesus.

Prayer: Lord, I pray that I love you with all of my heart, soul, mind, and strength. I want to love you with all of my love and loyalty; all of my identity; all that I think, decide, or desire; and all of my submission and effort. It is comforting to know that if I do my best, you will do the rest. In your greatness, you even equip me to love. Let me love my neighbor with pure love that runs from your heart through mine.

Care: Have you steered clear of certain ministries or missions because you thought *those people* didn't deserve to be served? You might think that people of other religions, or those who have made sinful life choices, are lost causes or not worth your time or money. Nothing could be farther from the truth. We must repent from all biases, preferences, and prejudices and see all people for who they are—as bearing the image of God and a soul for which Jesus died. Christ loves them as much as He loves you. Find an opportunity to serve a person or group that you once avoided or even judged. Show your love for God by sharing His love with them.

♻ **Share:** Jesus called us to love our neighbors as we love ourselves. Our sameness begins with our Creator, our heavenly Father whose image we bear. Share this with someone who feels like they never fit in—the person who sits alone, who deliberately makes their appearance stand out, or whose background would have them believe that you have nothing in common.

Section Three

ENEMIES TO
A LIFE OF LOVE

*And you were dead in the trespasses and sins in which you
once walked, following the course of this world, following
the prince of the power of the air, the spirit that is now at
work in the sons of disobedience—among whom we all once
lived in the passions of our flesh, carrying out the desires
of the body and the mind, and were by nature children of
wrath, like the rest of mankind.*

Ephesians 2:1-3

No military commander would go to war against an enemy
that he has not first scouted out. This was true all the way
back in Moses' time. It is not wise to seek to go to war without
first being aware of who you are up against.

Love is the greatest expression of God's kingdom on the
earth. Love is how we will see hearts won to Jesus Christ. Love
is how authentic discipleship will mold the next generation of
warriors for Jesus. Therefore it is clear that our spiritual enemy,
satan, will not allow us to advance in sacrificial love without a
fight. He has set up traps to try to derail us.

In Ephesians 2, Paul lists three very real enemies to a life
of love: "the course of this world," "the prince of the power of

the air," and "the passions of our flesh." Over the next six days, we are going to examine these enemies so that we are aware of them and so that we can see God's means of overcoming them.

We are not meant to live as victims. Our victory will not come through our own might and willpower, but through learning to rely more deeply on God's Spirit. Let's pray as we examine the enemies of our faith.

Father, I come before you in humility to acknowledge that there have been times when I have allowed myself to become a victim to my flesh, the world, and the devil. Today, I desire to understand what seeks to keep me from a life of love so that you can show me how to overcome. I thank you for a life of overcoming victory in advance.

Our Flesh Cannot Love

For the mind that is set on the flesh is hostile to God, for it does not submit to God's law; indeed, it cannot. Those who are in the flesh cannot please God.

Romans 8:7–8

EXPERIENCE GOD'S LOVE

Whether we realize it or not, our flesh is at war with God. The corrupt roots of our fleshly nature are wrapped in pride in ourselves and an unbelief in God's goodness. Our pride is so great that we think we know better than God does. Our unbelief is so deep that we would never trust God if it were not for His grace (Ephesians 2:8).

We were born selfish to the core. And the worst part about our selfish heart is that it makes it impossible to love others around us as we were created to love. Even with those who are closest to us, like our family and friends, we find that, in our own strength, we do not have the power to love them as we ought to.

How many times have you noticed irritation in yourself when things were not going your way? How many times have you given into anger, greed, lust, jealousy, sloth, and gluttony in order to pacify your flesh? The catch is, trying harder to overcome our flesh does not work. In order to live a life of victory, our flesh must die through our surrender to God.

In most areas of our physical lives, if we fail at something, all we need to do is try harder and eventually we can succeed. Think of the many athletes who have put in extra hours of practice and gone from the bench to becoming star players. How many students have learned that if they study harder they can go from failing to succeeding?

Yet this approach is not true of the spiritual battle we are in. In fact, the harder we try to overcome in our own strength, the more obvious it becomes that we do not have the necessary spiritual power in ourselves. It is only as we have a revelation of just how good God is, and that He is for us and not against us, that we will surrender our lives over to Him. As we surrender and trust Him, this releases His Spirit to set us free.

Father, I thank you that you are greater than my sinful nature. I ask for your forgiveness for the many times that I have chosen to submit to my flesh rather than submitting to your leadership of my life. Today, as an act of my will, I fully submit to you, and I trust you to overcome everything that I could not.

EXPRESS GOD'S LOVE

Do you ever feel like there is a war going on inside of you? Do you ever debate over a decision that has you pulled between something you think will be fun or fulfilling but deep down inside you know it is selfish or sinful? Our flesh is weak, but the Spirit makes our soul strong. Nothing we do in the flesh, even "good deeds," pleases God. He is not impressed when we strike out on our own, when we make decisions without consulting Him, or when we work in our own strength, exercising pride instead of prayer. Stop what you are doing and pray; experience the Spirit's strength in you and experience success instead of frustration. Give Jesus all the glory as people notice your growth and gain.

👤 **Prayer:** Holy Spirit, I cannot accomplish anything without you. Even my "righteous acts are like filthy rags" without you (Isaiah 64:6). Make me your instrument of glory; in my weakness, let the world see your strength. In my foolishness, let the world be awed by your wisdom. I will not set my hand to do anything apart from you. I know that I am not "bothering" you in prayer for guidance and provision but I am honoring you as my God. Let my lips and life give you praise and thanks always.

♥ **Care:** People with disabilities amaze me (Kathy) with their strength and can-do attitudes. They are great glory givers, showing the world that the Holy Spirit enables them even when the flesh has failed them. Spend some time getting to know and serving with someone with special needs or a disability. Don't assume that they need your help, but get to know them and their family and look for ways to bless them. Watching their life will bless you.

♻ **Share:** Romans 8:6 says, "For to set the mind on the flesh is death, but to set the mind on the Spirit is life and peace." God gives you the option to make up your mind. You decide what you will follow, the flesh or the Spirit. God is clear: choosing to follow Him brings life and peace, but choosing the flesh is hostile. You cannot be neutral—if you are not for Him, you are against Him. Share this with someone you know or meet today who is looking for peace. The Prince of Peace has been pursuing them to offer life and peace today.

God's Grace Rescues Us from Our Flesh

We all once lived in the passions of our flesh, carrying out the desires of the body and the mind, and were by nature children of wrath, like the rest of mankind. But God, being rich in mercy, because of the great love with which he loved us, even when we were dead in our trespasses, made us alive together with Christ—by grace you have been saved.

Ephesians 2:3–5

EXPERIENCE GOD'S LOVE

Unmerited favor. We have a hard time understanding that in a performance-based society. Yet the Word of God boldly declares that our salvation has nothing to do with our performance but everything to do with God's grace.

It is God's rich mercy and His great love for us that makes us alive. It is solely and only by His grace that we have come to faith in Him and desire to live as Jesus did. It is solely and only because He is at work in us that we have the spiritual strength to walk in victory over the pride and unbelief of our flesh.

Pride and unbelief are like twin roots of our sin nature. They seek to keep us bound up in our sin and unable to live as Jesus has called us to. Like Paul, we too can declare, "Wretched man that I am! Who will deliver me from this body of death? Thanks be to God through Jesus Christ our Lord!" (Romans 7:24–25).

Christ offers you a full and sustained victory. This victory is available here and now over every sin and every scheme of the devil that you are presently facing. God desires that you experience His victory right here and now.

The deeper you submit yourself to the lordship of Jesus Christ, the more the power of pride will be broken off your life. The more you learn to trust God, the greater victory you will experience over unbelief. You will come to experience a real salvation from sin that surpasses anything your human efforts could ever have won for you. This victory is available to all of God's children, and it is His promise to you. Take Him up on His offer to set you free today.

Father, I thank you that you have already purchased the victory for me through the shed blood of your Son, Jesus Christ. Today I choose to enter into your victory by faith. I choose to submit to you, and I believe you to break the power of pride off my life. I choose to trust you, and I believe you will set me free from unbelief. Thank you for the freedom that you have made available to me right here and now. Use my life for your glory.

EXPRESS GOD'S LOVE

Soak in the fact that because of God's *great* love for you, He prepared the path to salvation for you. Before you took a breath, before you heard your first Scripture or sermon, before you professed faith, grace was waiting for your faith to take hold of it and blow open the gates of heaven and usher in abundant life for you. Let that fill you as you engage with people who need guiding toward the path to grace today.

Prayer: Lord, thank you for your great love and grace—it is truly amazing! Your heart for me paved the way for my sin-filled life to be cleansed and made useful for your kingdom. Thank you! When I meet someone who needs to know your grace, help me to be a person of grace and mercy since I received so much from you. (Remember to continue to pray for all of the people you listed on your Prayer-Care-Share lists.)

Care: Do you know someone who has made some bad choices with serious, life-changing consequences? How do they find their way to or back to Jesus? The guilt and shame can be blinding and binding, keeping them from believing that a church would ever open their doors, much less their arms, to them. Show them the way, and journey with them to a grace-filled church family who knows that Christians are not perfect but a work in progress. Ask God to draw your heart to someone who needs grace and to know about God's second chances.

⚠ **Share:** We may remember that grace brought us to Jesus, but sometimes we forget that this same unmerited favor is what equips and blesses us through life. We walk through the doors of abundant life by grace but somehow get turned around and start trying to earn favor, love, and blessings throughout life. Jesus could not love you any more than He does right now. You are a significant person with a significant kingdom purpose, and your faith in and love for Jesus is all you need to be showered with blessings and opportunities that will enable you to fulfill your destiny. Share this with someone who struggles with insecurity or works-based religion; your faith-filled relationship is the key to God's heart.

The World
Does Not Know Love

The god of this world has blinded the minds of the unbeliev-
ers, to keep them from seeing the light of the gospel of the
glory of Christ, who is the image of God.

2 Corinthians 4:4

EXPERIENCE GOD'S LOVE

The world around us is knowingly or unknowingly chasing after
love at a breakneck pace. People are trying to get their hands on
anything they can to fill themselves with some form of life. From
the latest digital device, to their latest social media post, to the
latest restaurant, to the latest vehicle. There are simply so many
things competing for our worship.

You see, anything we turn to for life outside of God is an
idol. This can even include seemingly good things like family and
friends. Our God is a God of love, and in His love He is also a
jealous God. Let me explain. He does not want anyone or anything competing for our deepest affections. Just as a husband
expects his wife to only express physical intimacy with him and
no one else, God expects us to find our deepest spiritual satisfaction solely in Him.

Is it possible that there is something in your life today that you have allowed to become an idol? Is there anything that you consistently turn to for life outside of Christ? God desires all of your heart. He wants to be the one and only person, place, or thing that you look to for life. Jesus said, "This is eternal life, that they know you, the only true God, and Jesus Christ whom you have sent" (John 17:3). Today you can experience an abundance of life in Jesus that makes all the pleasures of earth pale in comparison. Do you believe that?

Take a moment and allow God's Spirit to speak to your heart. *Father, I ask you to show me any areas of my life where I have turned to other things for life outside of you.* (Wait and give Him time to speak to you.)

The truth is that choosing idols comes from the root sin of choosing to be the leader of your own life. God's Spirit does not turn to idols, and you will not either, if He is truly in control. The repentance that God desires is for us to change our mind about who is leading our life. As you repent by surrendering fully to Christ's leadership, His supernatural empowerment will fill you with the strength to overcome.

> *Father, I confess that I have allowed idols in my heart. I agree with you that turning to _____ (be specific) for life, instead of turning to you for life, has been a sin that has grieved you. By your grace, I change my mind regarding who is the leader of my life. I no longer want to be the leader. I ask you to lead my every thought, word, and action. I thank you right now for taking over my life with your life.*

EXPRESS GOD'S LOVE

One of the greatest life lessons I (Kathy) have ever learned is "You don't know what you don't know." We make decisions, assumptions, and judgments sometimes based on partial knowledge and surface evidence only to find out later how wrong we are. I remember a dear principal who confided in me for prayer for his cancer diagnosis that he was keeping quiet. Doctor's appointments and chemo interrupted his school days; meanwhile, an acquaintance of mine kept popping in to try to see him. She began to gossip and grumble about him, accusing him of everything from an affair to job interviews. I bit my tongue and suggested she make an appointment instead of dropping by, but she continued to spread rumors all over our district. Imagine her embarrassment when she learned about his cancer battle. Let grace set the pace of your life.

Prayer: Lord, give me eyes to see you and all of your wonderful works going on around me. Give me your eyes to see people the way you see them. Take any blinders off, and help me to remember that unbelievers cannot behave as those who know you and your Word—they don't know what they don't know. Remind me to behave as I profess to believe. Let me walk in love and lead others to you.

Care: Has the behavior of someone you know changed lately? Are they acting out of character or distant? Go to them today and ask, "Are we okay?" And if they say yes, ask them, "Are you okay?" Do not let them dodge your questions. Look them in the eyes with great compassion and tell them how much they mean to you.

♻ **Share:** Do you have any friends who are unbelievers? Sometimes we isolate ourselves with our church friends and small groups; we go to our Christian bookstores and coffee shops and have no idea what is going on with the people we were sent to lead to love. It is important to have close Christian friends and support Christian businesses, films, and radio, but we cannot close ourselves off from our mission field. Connect with someone new at work, school, or in your neighborhood that you do not believe knows Jesus and get to know them. Ask God to use you to help take the enemy's blinders off so they can see the light of the gospel of the glory of Christ.

Our Faith
Overcomes the World

For everyone who has been born of God overcomes the world. And this is the victory that has overcome the world—our faith.

1 John 5:4

EXPERIENCE GOD'S LOVE

Salmon have an amazing feature that God built into them. When they hatch, salmon swim downstream into the ocean where they mature. After a number of years, they return to the original hatching place in order to lay and fertilize their eggs. The difficulty is, to get back to where they started, they have to swim against the current. In many locations this involves literally jumping over waterfalls and rapids that are flowing in the opposite direction. Only the strong survive, while many die trying.

In a similar way, we live at a time when the belief system of the world is like a strong current flowing in the opposite direction of the will of God. This stream of anti-Christ beliefs has caused a great dilemma for God's people around the world. Sadly, many who claim Christ have allowed the pressures and pleasures of the world to knock them off track to such a degree that they are being pushed in the opposite direction of the kingdom of God.

This verse in 1 John reminds us that our victory over the world comes through our faith in God. When we fill ourselves with what God has said is pure, right, and true, like an eagle, we begin to rise above the current of the world. It is possible through our faith in God, and through our obedience to the promptings of His Spirit, to become so separated from the way of life the world values that we have authority over it. Just as an eagle could easily fly over a stream of water without even being touched by it.

Is the way of the world pushing you in the opposite direction of God? If so, you do not need to allow this to continue to happen. Even now you can choose to step toward God with a deeper measure of faith. You can ask Him to set you free from the pressures and temptations of this world, so that you can be effective in reaching out to others who have been caught in the world's stream.

Father, I thank you that you are greater than the pressures and temptations the world seeks to bring against me. By faith I lay hold of you. Today I ask you to set me apart from the belief system of this world so that I will value the things that you value. I submit my life to you. Help me to make the right decisions regarding what I allow and what I do not allow into my life. Set me free and use me for your glory to rescue many other souls.

EXPRESS GOD'S LOVE

Jesus has overcome! Joy and courage should erupt from your heart as you think about what that statement means as a follower of Jesus. You walk in the power and authority of the One who has overcome death and offers eternal life—abundant life that begins now as you are forever changed and being transformed into the character of Christ. Exercise that authority over the enemy; show the world what it means to live and love in victory.

Prayer: Lord, thank you for life! Thank you for defeating the enemy and filling me with your Spirit, equipping me to battle with love and turn heads and hearts to you. Keep me steadfast in your love so that I may not be tripped or tangled up in temptation or deception. Keep my path clear, that I may not stumble into satan's snares. Let me take your love across the street and around the world through the people and places you put in my path, always for your glory.

Care: We not only want to overcome culture; we also want to overwhelm culture with the love and message of Jesus. It is not just that we want darkness defeated; we want Christ's light to shine with hope and the sovereignty of Jesus. We want love to replace hate, courage to replace fear, unity to replace division, compassion to replace indifference. Love is a verb that marches and moves to overcome evil and bring victory to those who would otherwise be swallowed in despair and darkness. It is not just about avoiding evil and temptation but about the victory of love and light.

⚠ **Share:** When we think about sharing the gospel, we often think of a mission trip to a foreign land. These are significant trips; but so are the walks you take to your neighbor's house. *Every* soul matters to Jesus. You live, work, learn, shop, dine, work out, and hang out in certain places by God's design. You are on mission every day. Know that there are dozens if not hundreds of international students in the colleges and universities not far from your home. Introducing them to the love and life in Christ while they are in your community could result in their returning to their country to spread the gospel with their influence and education. Look for ways to share Jesus around the world by looking around your community.

Battle in
the Heavenly Places

*For we do not wrestle against flesh and blood, but against
the rulers, against the authorities, against the cosmic powers over this present darkness, against the spiritual forces of
evil in the heavenly places.*

Ephesians 6:12

EXPERIENCE GOD'S LOVE

A boxer takes months to prepare for his next match. He lifts
weights, runs, spars, and eats well to prepare. Moments before
going into the ring, his trainer tells him, "I forgot to mention this
to you, but your opponent is invisible." The boxer laughs, thinking this is just a joke. When he gets into the ring, he doesn't see
anyone in the opposite corner. The referee comes out and starts
the match, and before he has a chance to swing, the boxer is pum-
meled from all sides by an unseen enemy. Blood is flowing from
his forehead and jaw as he staggers back to his corner, barely
avoiding a knockout in the first round.

Sadly, this is the situation many sincere Christ followers find
themselves in. For whatever reason, no one thought to mention
to us that we have an invisible enemy. In other cases, we may have

been told, but we didn't really believe it. One of satan's great lies in the Western world is that he does not exist.

Without a revelation from God, it is easy to believe that our enemy is the people around us who appear to be causing us difficulties. If we do not know who our true enemy is, we can easily fall into the trap of fighting against "flesh and blood." In this way, we lose our ability to love as God intends us to. How can we love those we view as our enemies?

Paul makes it clear that our true enemy is in the "heavenly places." No human being will ever be your enemy. Natural ways of fighting are useless against spiritual forces of evil. Self-protection and withdrawal. Anger and verbal debates. Unforgiveness, bitterness, and gossip. Like a man attempting to hit satan by swinging his fist in the air, these methods are futile.

Have you ever wondered why your method of fighting satan is not working? Recognize that your true battle is spiritual. Instead of relying on human tactics, learn to go on your knees in prayer. This battle is the Lord's (2 Chronicles 20:15). As you rely on Him in prayer, He will fight the spiritual forces of evil that have come against you. As you learn to keep in step with God's Spirit, no weapon formed against you will prosper (Isaiah 54:17).

Father, I thank you for revealing to me that the true battle is spiritual. Forgive me for the times when I have treated people as though they were my enemy. By your grace, teach me to fight where it counts. Teach me to engage in the battle in the spiritual realm through prayer. Thank you in advance for the victory that you will bring about as I continue to trust in you.

EXPRESS GOD'S LOVE

It is important to understand that all of the wars, hatred, and pain in the world are a reflection of the invisible battles for souls going on between God's kingdom and satan. Do not ever think that it is an equal fight; God is far superior to the created fallen angel we know as satan and his fallen army, but every person gets to choose who they will follow and fight for. Satan fights dirty and wants to bring death and destruction wherever he goes. We must fight with fervent prayer and love; the enemy cannot fight against them. Whenever you encounter conflict, cruelty, or crisis, ask the Holy Spirit to fill the space and situation with His presence and provision. Never hate people; hate the enemy who has blinded them.

Prayer: Lord, forgive me for my negative thoughts and feelings toward people you sent me to pray for and love. (Think about certain people or situations in your life that are hurtful or hate filled and pray about them now. Pray for someone who has hurt you deeply. Pray unity over division, humility over pride, and healing over woundedness.)

Care: Isolation is more than loneliness; it can be an emotional playground for satan. When I (Kathy) was sick with a brain tumor, my hardest days were when I was stuck home alone, thinking about the burden I was on my family, the sorrow I was causing them and that they would be better off without me. I can call out the lies of the accuser now, but isolation twists your perception since we were meant to live in relationship and community. Do you know of an elderly person or someone who is ill in your neighborhood or church family who cannot get out much or at all? Go visit them, and make it a habit to go by and check on them and chat. Connect them with the love and care they need to receive.

⚓ **Share:** Jesus said, "The thief comes only to steal and kill and destroy; I came that they may have life, and have it abundantly" (John 10:10 NASB). If you are involved or know about a situation where happiness, health, relationship, and destiny is under attack, go encourage the people involved to see the enemy's trap that they have fallen into and the destruction that lies ahead for both or all of them. Blessed are the peacemakers (Matthew 5:9).

Loving God Overcomes the Enemy

"God opposes the proud but gives grace to the humble."
Submit yourselves therefore to God. Resist the devil, and he
will flee from you.

James 4:6–7

EXPERIENCE GOD'S LOVE

James gives us a clear prescription for victory in every situation. Have you been beaten down by spiritual opposition? Has the enemy been having a heyday in your personal life, marriage, and family? Look no further. The Word of God has an immediate cure that will work every time if we apply it from our hearts.

The prescription is simple and has only two parts. Submit to God. Resist the devil. The end result is that satan will flee from you. He will flee from that person or situation that concerns you. If you will do these two things, then you are truly handing the battle over to God. And God wins every time. In fact, He has not lost a single spiritual confrontation in all of human history, and He never will.

Now before we presume we are already putting this into practice, let's take a closer look at what this really means. Today let's allow God's Spirit to give us a fresh awareness of whether or not we are living in submission to Him. To subject ourselves to someone is to obey them. Are we truly surrendering ourselves to full obedience to God's Spirit? If not, let's renew our surrender and willingness to obey right now.

The word translated *resist* in the original Greek means "to take a complete stand against, to forcefully declare one's personal conviction; to ardently withstand without giving up."[7] Based on that definition, are you really taking a stand against the enemy, or are you dabbling with the temptations he brings your way? Are you forcefully declaring your conviction regarding the ways of God, or are you allowing for subtle compromise, and even at times inviting satan into your life? If you have not truly been resisting the enemy through the decisions of your will, take a forceful stand today, and determine by the power of His Spirit to hold unswervingly to God's ways.

Surrender to God. Invite the power of His Spirit to give you the grace to resist the enemy. Then stand and watch as God wins the victory.

Father, today I come to you to refresh the full surrender of my life to you. Forgive me for holding on to areas of my life and not truly allowing you to be in control. I fully submit every area of my life to you right now. I also ask for your forgiveness for not truly resisting evil but at times allowing it to have room in my life. Today, by your grace, I choose to resist the enemy. I reject his will and his ways in my life. Instead, I choose your will and your ways in every area of my life. I thank you that your Word says that the enemy will flee from me and that your victory is certain.

7 Strong, *Strong's Exhaustive Concordance of the Bible*, s.v. "resist." http://biblehub .com/greek/436.htm (accessed April 9, 2017).

EXPRESS GOD'S LOVE

It is human nature to cast blame away from ourselves when we get caught or get caught up in sin. The old excuse, "The devil made me do it," does not fly because the devil only tempts; he cannot *make* you do anything. How empowering to read in Scripture that we can make him do something—we can make him flee. Pride opens the door for him, while humility closes it. Flirting with sin draws closer to satan, but submitting to God makes the enemy scram. If you want to see him run faster, start praising and thanking Jesus.

👤 **Prayer:** Lord, I praise you as my Creator, Savior, and Master; the love and deliverer of my soul. I want to enter your gates with thanksgiving and your courts with praise and remain there all day long. My heart longs to dwell in your presence faraway from the enemy. I submit to you my attitude, affections, and actions. Keep my foot from stumbling and send the devil running. You are my refuge and my King.

❤ **Care:** There are times when people who we love need us to help them resist the devil. He is not creative—he finds our weakness, our insecurity, and he will pull the same trick over and over again. If you know someone with a specific temptation, let them know that they can call you in an emergency, that you will come and get them or come be with them to fight through the struggle in prayer and submission to God's will and ways. Whether it is your friend, family member, even your own teenager, they need to know that they have a way out of temptation, that they are never stranded with satan. You cannot be their Savior, but you can help keep them safe.

⛅ **Share:** God's plan is the very best for you, greater than anything you can dream or imagine. Satan has a plan for your life too. Have you ever thought about that? For everything God does, satan has a counterfeit. Satan is your enemy, not your buddy. You know someone who needs to hear this today. The enemy has a battle plan against your destiny; if he can't steal your soul, he will steal as many blessings as possible. Remember to resist him, and bless God and let Him fight for you while you submit to Him.

SPIRITUAL KEYS TO REMAIN IN GOD'S LOVE

For this reason I bow my knees before the Father, from whom every family in heaven and on earth is named, that according to the riches of his glory he may grant you to be strengthened with power through his Spirit in your inner being, so that Christ may dwell in your hearts through faith—that you, being rooted and grounded in love, may have strength to comprehend with all the saints what is the breadth and length and height and depth, and to know the love of Christ that surpasses knowledge, that you may be filled with all the fullness of God.

Ephesians 3:14–19

A heart of full surrender and complete trust in God is the foundation of a life that is lived for the glory of God. How do we fight to remain in a place of real surrender and deep trust? How do we remain in a place of choosing to sacrificially love others? What about when people and circumstances seek to push us out of a place of surrender and trust in God's Spirit? What about the pressure of the world's system and the spiritual forces of wickedness in the heavenly places? How can we possibly be expected to stand and choose God's will and ways in the face of such tremendous opposition?

As followers of Jesus Christ, we all desire to live overcoming lives. At the same time, for many believers, we have sought to overcome the temptations of our flesh, the world, and the enemy through our own willpower, and it simply has not worked. We have made renewed commitments to never give in to that habitual sin again, only to find that within a short period of time, we are tripped up again. What is God's solution? Is freedom from sin even possible?

What if instead of focusing on the areas of sin we are struggling with, we tried a radically different approach? What if we sought to so focus our lives on God, and allow His Spirit to so fill us, that there was no room in our lives for sin? What if we put into place an ongoing lifestyle of waiting on God, filling ourselves with His Word, worship, prayer, and engaging with other believers at a depth of fellowship that we remain deeply grounded in the life of Christ? Do you think that this radically different approach would bear much better fruit than what we have seen in the past?

Instead of turning to the sinful areas you have been struggling with and seeking to use your own strength to overcome, this next section of the book encourages you to allow God's Spirit to build a lifestyle in you that leaves no room for the enemy to have a foothold. By God's grace, He has given us practical, spiritual keys that we can put into practice in our daily lives, which will unlock a depth of intimacy with God that is fresh and sustainable. We are going to examine five of these spiritual keys over the next ten days. Through the empowerment of God, we can use these practical tools to remain in a place where Christ's life and love is flowing in us and through us at all times.

A Lifestyle
of Praise and Worship:
God Is Seeking Worshipers

*"The hour is coming, and is now here, when the true wor-
shipers will worship the Father in spirit and truth, for the
Father is seeking such people to worship him.",*

John 4:23

EXPERIENCE GOD'S LOVE

A man stands, hands in his pockets, lips barely moving, as a
worship song plays from the stage. It is not his lack of physical
movement that is the true problem. It is a heart that is not truly
engaged. Three hours later, this same man is jumping and shout-
ing with his hands reaching skyward. His favorite sports team
just made the winning play.

The truth is, we are going to worship something. God made
us to worship. The question is, will our true worship be directed
to God?

Even now, God is searching the earth for people who will
worship Him in spirit and truth. God is not merely looking for
those who will sing a few songs and give lip service to Him, but
those who will live with their lives wide open to Him, giving Him

thanks at all times. God is seeking wholehearted worshipers. All over the earth they are streaming into His kingdom—the former drug addicts, prostitutes, and witch doctors who now bow at the feet of Jesus and give Him the worship that He is so worthy of. How about you? Do you live a life of truly worshiping God at all times?

Elsewhere, Jesus warns us that, "He who is forgiven little, loves little" (Luke 7:47). The truth is, we have all been forgiven far more than we can even imagine. The real issue is that some of us have forgotten how much we have been forgiven, or perhaps we have never had a revelation of the depth of our sinfulness. If we could see how much we have been forgiven, we would love extravagantly.

Religious traditions can also be a hindrance, teaching us man's ideas of what is acceptable and unacceptable worship. Notice that this passage does not specify a form of worship but that the focus is on the heart. God does not want us judging each other for the different outward ways in which we choose to worship. God sees if we are really worshiping Him from our hearts.

The worship that God seeks is far more than a few weekly services. He desires hearts that are learning to worship Him at all times. In order to remain deeply connected to Jesus, a lifestyle of continuous praise and worship is essential. Take a moment to wait on God and ask, "How would you have me grow in wholehearted worship of you?"

Father, I ask you for a deeper revelation of just how much you have forgiven me, so that I may live a life of continuous worship. I ask that you show me any way religious traditions are keeping me from worshiping you freely. Today, I ask you to teach me to worship you with my whole heart.

EXPRESS GOD'S LOVE

Worship is not just a Sunday morning or church thing; it is an all-day, everyday lifestyle. Today's verse is part of a conversation between Jesus and the woman at the well. She is wondering why Jesus would speak to her since Jews despised the Samaritans and saw them as "unworthy" to worship God at the temple. Jesus reveals that God is more concerned about where the worship comes from, not where it takes place; God wants pure, passionate worship from the heart, not lip service from legalism.

Prayer: Lord, you alone are worthy of my worship. I want my life to be lived in worship; not just in songs but in prayer, living out your love with great care and sharing your message with people far and near without fear. Let my giving, my conversation, the way I dress, talk, and live all worship you Sunday through Saturday, in spirit and in truth.

Care: There are so many ways to worship Jesus. The arts and entertainment industry is filled with people who want to use their gifts and talents to spark conversations about faith, to point people to the majesty of the Creator and not just the beauty of His creation. They express worship on the screen and stage not just in the church building. Pray for the Christians who work to fight the darkness in these industries; bless and don't curse them as they seek to glorify God. Go to the movies that are faith and family friendly; invest in, support, share, and applaud their work. Take someone to see a faith-based film and then listen to their response as the film opens the door to a faith-based discussion.

⛅ **Share:** Church is just one place where we worship, but it is also a vital part of worship. Corporate prayer, learning, singing, giving, and fellowship are an essential part of being a Christ follower. We are stronger together, we accomplish more together, and we are supported and grow like a vine intertwined, together. The church is not perfect; the Holy Spirit is working in us and through us, but He is not finished with us. I like the saying, "The church is a hospital for sinners, not a museum for saints." Someone who has been hurt by the church or who has never been to church needs you to share this with them today.

A Lifestyle
of Praise and Worship:
Give Thanks at All Times

*Rejoice always, pray without ceasing, give thanks in all cir-
cumstances; for this is the will of God in Christ Jesus for you.*
1 Thessalonians 5:16–18

EXPERIENCE GOD'S LOVE

I (Chris) had the privilege of spending time with a Ugandan mis-
sionary to the United States named Nicodemus. Nicodemus was
one of the most unique men I have ever met. He was a man of
continuous prayer and praise. Often when we would be walking
down the street, looking through a store, or in a room full of people, he was praying and singing praise songs to God. He truly
exemplified a person who understood that we are to give thanks
in every circumstance.

One day, Nicodemus was onboard an overcrowded boat in
the middle of a massive lake between Uganda and Tanzania. A
huge storm came up out of nowhere and began beating against
the boat, threatening to knock it over. Nicodemus had never
learned to swim. As the waves were crashing against the boat in
a rhythmic fashion, Nicodemus turned to his companion and
declared, "Look, even the wind and the waves are clapping and

giving praise to God!" Nicodemus proceeded to worship the Lord.

How about you? Have you learned the secret of giving thanks to God in all circumstances? Or do you allow the people and circumstances in your life to push you down? Does your faith, hope, and love change based on your circumstances? If so, then you have not yet learned to "rejoice always" and "give thanks in all circumstances."

What frees us to rejoice and give thanks at all times is when our hearts have had a revelation of the sovereignty of God. When we realize that God is able to take even the events that appear tragic to us and use them for His glory, then we are freed to trust Him at all times. When we have a rock-solid assurance of God's character, then we have the spiritual fortitude to choose to rejoice at all times.

In this place of joy, when we continually acknowledge the sovereignty and goodness of God in every circumstance, love flows freely toward all people. We are freed to see even the hardest souls with His compassion. In this way, our lifestyle of praise and worship gives great glory to God.

In order to remain deeply connected to Jesus, a lifestyle of continuous praise and worship is essential. Take a moment to wait on God and ask, "How do you desire me to grow in a lifestyle of giving thanks and praise to you at all times?"

Father, I ask for your forgiveness for the times when I have allowed negative thinking and negative speech to overtake me. I thank you that through the power of your Holy Spirit, it is possible to live a life of thanksgiving and praise at all times. Remove everything that would keep me from choosing to give you the praise you deserve. Today I choose to give you thanks for _____ (be specific).

EXPRESS GOD'S LOVE

We have to be careful that we do not misread or misrepresent the Scriptures; the enemy miscues us with, "Did God really say …?" or by slipping words in and out to change the meaning. (For example, it is not *money* that is the root of all evil, but the *love* of money.) Today's verse is often misquoted as "give thanks *for* all circumstances" instead of "*in* all circumstances." I love how Chris' friend found rhythm in the waves and wind and praised God through the storm but not necessarily for the storm.

Growth comes from storms. We can be wise and choose to grow in our faith, steadfastness, wisdom, and knowledge, or we can be foolish and grow the gap between us and those things by complaining and compromising our faith and character. Praise Him in the storm and in the sunshine. Rejoice always.

Prayer: Lord, thank you for walking on the waves; as the storm blew and the sea roared, you trampled the waves and revealed your glory. Reveal your glory to me through the storms of life. Grow me and guide me as I place every breath in your hands and trust you with the life that you gave to me. My life and destiny are yours; I am your disciple and servant.

Care: Have you ever prayed or done something kind for a police officer, firefighter, or paramedic? These are the people who go running into dangerous places when everyone else is running away. You depend on them to protect you and your property; you expect them at your doorstep just moments after dialing 9-1-1. Show care and appreciation for them every time you have an opportunity; buy them coffee, a meal, or even bake them something or go thank them personally if they live in your neighborhood. Always pray for them and their families when you pass them on the road or see them drive through your neighborhood.

⛅ **Share:** Has there ever been an emergency in your neighborhood—a fire, ambulance, or police car in someone's driveway? Every neighborhood has moments of crisis and celebrations—everything from garage sales to graduations, robberies, deaths, and weather-related outages or destruction. Consider starting a Prayer-Care-Share hub in your neighborhood that prays together, watches out for one another, and responds with love in times of triumph and tragedy.

A Lifestyle of Waiting and Listening to God's Spirit: God's Children Hear His Voice

"My sheep hear my voice, and I know them, and they fol-low me."

John 10:27

EXPERIENCE GOD'S LOVE

Picture yourself coming before a king. This is not just any king but the King of Kings and the Lord of Lords. As you are escorted into the room, you realize He is seated on a glorious throne. Now imagine perfect white light emanating from the King throughout the room. Off to His side are huge angelic beings continuously singing, "Holy, holy, holy, is the Lord God Almighty, who was and is and is to come!" (Revelation 4:8).

What would you do in that moment? What would you say? Would you go into a long monologue? Would you list off all the problems you are going through? Or would you fall on your face in awe of Him and be silent?

When we are standing before the being who created us and who knows all things, who do you think should be the one doing most of the talking? Remember Moses falling on his face continually before God, and remember Isaiah declaring he was "a man of unclean lips" (Isaiah 6:5)? Remember King David stating, "Who am I, O Lord God, and what is my house, that you have brought me thus far?" (2 Samuel 7:18)?

Three separate times in John 10, Jesus tells us that His children hear and know His voice. Do you know the voice of God? Have you taken the time to wait and listen to Him to such a degree that you can discern His voice from the other voices that are seeking to speak to you? If not, now is the time. Jesus has given you a promise that you can know His voice, and He expects you to take the time to learn to hear His direction.

God can speak to us in many ways. Through the Word of God, through prayer, through circumstances, through people. The important thing is learning to surrender our will to Him and then to discern exactly what He is saying. He is the author of communication, and He desires to make His will known to us even more than we desire to know it. Therefore, we can trust Him to speak to us with clarity.

In order to remain deeply connected to Christ, a lifestyle of waiting and listening to God's Spirit is essential. Take a moment now to put this into practice.

Father, I thank you that you promise me in your Word that your children hear your voice. I desire to learn to hear your voice more than I ever have before. Today I ask you to speak to me. (Take time to wait on Him now, believing that He will speak to you.)

EXPRESS GOD'S LOVE

God gave you the ability to communicate; He gave you the ability to hear and the ability to talk. If we were created for Him, by Him, then why would we think that He would not talk to us? God talks to you; it just takes practice to listen. God's voice will never contradict His Word, and He will not bring up guilt from forgiven sin—that voice is the accuser. Listen carefully.

👤 **Prayer:** Lord, I am your sheep, you are my Good Shepherd. I want to hear your voice, over the noise of this world and my own desires and thoughts. Help me to be quiet, to still my life and listen to you with my soul. Teach me to listen. Speak your love and lessons into my heart so that I can follow you all the days of my life.

♥ **Care:** This world is loud. We hurry about and stick earbuds in our ears to talk on our phones or play music. Silence is something we have to deliberately seek out. It has become so infrequent in our world that we feel uncomfortable or out of place in silence. Have you ever turned the television on just to have noise in the room? Give the gift of silence today: Invite a friend or your spouse to go somewhere quiet, such as a lake, on a hike, even your own backyard, and agree not to talk for at least thirty minutes. Clear your mind, don't think about work or schedules, just be still and quiet. Listen for God as you rest silently.

☁ **Share:** We have become a society that cannot sit still and be quiet. The average smartphone user reaches for their phones more than 2,617 times per day, with that number exceeding 5,000 for the heaviest cell phone users.[8] We are working but we are usually looking to see what the rest of the world is saying on social media, text, email, and more. Make it a habit to post something on your social media that is glorifying. Post Scripture, a praise of God's blessing, or a beautiful picture and thank God for His creation or the event in the picture. Use your voice to share God's words with someone searching their phone or tablet for inspiration or hope, but never enlist yourself to be a substitute for the voice of God. Pray for people and ask God to speak to them so that they hear and know His voice.

---

8   http://www.networkworld.com/article/3092446/smartphones/we-touch-our-phones-2617-times-a-day-says-study.html

A Lifestyle of Waiting and Listening to God's Spirit: Be Still

"Be still, and know that I am God. I will be exalted among the nations, I will be exalted in the earth!"

Psalm 46:10

EXPERIENCE GOD'S LOVE

The noise in our world can be deafening. From the television and the radio to the Internet and the latest billboards, all screaming for our attention. Just simply walking through a store or a restaurant, our senses are bombarded by screen after screen and message after message of what we should consider important. Is it any wonder that those who have learned to be still and listen to God are a minority among us?

Many tell me one of their greatest struggles in learning to listen to God is simply taking the time to hear from Him. Others who have learned to stop and listen often confess that the vast array of "to-dos" running through their minds is all they can seem to hear.

Relax. God is in control. He "will be exalted among the nations"; He "will be exalted in the earth!" Cease striving. Be still.

Take your to-do list and place it at the feet of Jesus. Then begin to cultivate a lifestyle of waiting and listening to what His Holy Spirit has to say to you.

Try it right now. Take everything that is on your mind and give it over to Jesus in prayer now.

When you have completed that, ask Him, "Father, I believe that you desire to speak to me even more than I desire to listen. Is there anything that you desire to say to me right now?"

After asking Him this question, pause, and wait as long as you need, until He speaks to you.

Once you have completed this exercise, begin to incorporate this as a regular part of your time spent with God. As you put this into practice on a regular basis, I trust that waiting on God will become one of the highlights of your daily life. Remember, He is the source of all life, and the deeper you connect with Him, the more fulfilling your life will be.

To remain deeply connected to Christ, a lifestyle of waiting and listening to God's Spirit is essential. Take a moment and express to God your desire to grow in this area.

Father, I thank you that you desire deep communion with me. Thank you for teaching me about waiting and listening to you. Show me how to put this into practice on a daily basis so that I will learn to hear more clearly from you. Thank you in advance for the peace and joy that I will experience in our relationship as I set aside time to listen to you.

EXPRESS GOD'S LOVE

Did you take my advice yesterday—were you able to give the gift of quietness to yourself and another person? Life is busy. If you did not get away yesterday, plan for quietness in the next few days. You have to seek it out, unless you spend a lot of time alone, and then the silence is deafening, even painful at times. Realize that you are never alone; God is always with you, a constant companion who loves the sound of your voice. He gave you that voice. You must make use of the quiet times; God has given some more than others, but no matter how full or empty your house may seem, take time to be still and seek Him. Give Him your full attention and praise Him as God—your God.

♟ Prayer: Lord, I know you are God. I believe it with my whole heart, and I want my life to exhibit my faith in you. You tell me to be still—the translation is to cease striving and to rest in the fact that you are the sovereign supremacy of my life and the universe. Let that sink into my heart and mind; bring me peace in your power. I surrender my struggles and submit to your will and your resolutions so that I can live out the destiny you planned for me in joy and faithfulness.

♥ Care: Are you pressing someone for a quick decision? Stop. Give that person some space and tell them you want them to pray about it. Do not push or persuade. You want God's will in everything you do, every direction that you take. Pray for them while you wait. Be still and know that He is able to speak to them and set your feet on the path that is best.

⛅ **Share:** As Christ followers we profess faith in the all-power-ful, all-loving, all-knowing God, but if we still freak out in challenges and crises, we are not testifying to the strength and peace that comes from a relationship with Him. In disaster, a diagnosis, disease, damaged relationships, whatever your storm or situation, trust God with a peace that is beyond the under-standing of everyone who is watching you. Be still and know … and show His love and strength in all circumstances. Share this promise of peace with someone who is jumping to conclusions and racing toward disaster. Be still and know.

A Lifestyle of Being Filled with the Word of God: The Word of God Sets Us Free

So Jesus said to the Jews who had believed him, "If you abide in my word, you are truly my disciples, and you will know the truth, and the truth will set you free."

John 8:31–32

EXPERIENCE GOD'S LOVE

A young couple in Henan Province, China, became Christians and participated in an "unregistered" congregation. Their hunger to grow in their newfound faith was incredible. At their house, all they had available were a few tattered pages from the book of John. They would read these over and over again, asking for God's wisdom. Just by keeping these pages in their house, they risked imprisonment by the local authorities. They determined it was worth the risk to grow in their knowledge of God.

Contrast that testimony with the lifestyle of many in the Western world. With Bibles available to us in print, electronic, audio, and visual formats, how many of us fail to take the time to fill ourselves with His Word? Jesus stated that His food was to do the will of God (John 4:34) and that He only spoke what He heard from His Father (John 12:49). The Word of God reveals the will of God to us. It is our daily spiritual sustenance. The truth found in God's Word sets us free. Sometimes we can fall into a trap of busyness and neglect the truth. Rather than taking the Word of God and slowly chewing on it, digesting it, and allowing its truth to permeate our souls, we may grab a snack-sized portion and quickly gobble it down before rushing out the door.

Are you leaving yourself adequate time to really feast on the Word of God on a daily basis? Are you trying to survive on snack-sized portions of the Word of God rather than taking the time for a full meal? While some of the Word of God is better than nothing, don't settle for less than God is offering you. Take the time. Make the time. We need God's truth to daily fill us and protect us from the lies of the enemy. If our brothers and sisters in China are willing to risk being imprisoned and killed for a scrap of God's Word, recognize the value that you have in your hands and feast on the Words of God.

A lifestyle of being filled with God's Word is essential to living deeply connected to Christ. Ask God's Spirit, "How do you want me to feast on your Word even more than I am presently doing?"

Father, I thank you for making your Word available to me. I ask for your forgiveness for times when I have neglected your Word. Today, I choose to make your Word a priority in my life. (Be specific about how you intend to put this into practice.)

EXPRESS GOD'S LOVE

Jesus tells His followers to abide in His Word, which means to continue and not depart from God's will, instructions, and the reality of the way God sees things. If you abide in His Word, the result is that you will be set free from the dominion of sin. Simply put, live in the way that God created you to live, filled with His Word and Spirit, and you will not be deceived or destroyed by sin.

Prayer: Lord, thank you for your Word and for giving us truth—the reality of how we should see and respond to every person, temptation, and circumstance. Thank you for setting us free so that we can abide with you forever. Continue to teach me to do your will. I am your disciple, your pupil, and I abide in your presence to know your Word and will.

Care: The only way to abide in God's Word is to open it, read it, study it, and then do it. You need to be in a Bible study that gives you a consistent learning and growing knowledge of the Bible. Invite a friend to join a Bible study with you or consider starting a Bible study in your neighborhood. Be sure that you have a mature, reliable teacher so that you learn and abide in truth. Never be afraid to say, "I don't know, but let's find out" if someone asks a question and you do not know the answer. You do not want to cause someone to abide in misinformation.

Share: Having God's Word in your heart and on your mind is the best way to stay joyful, hopeful, and away from sin. Knowing His Word and understanding the application will prepare you to share His Word with others, give godly counsel, and convey God's truth instead of guessing what is right or giving personal opinions. When you share His Word, always be willing to have someone check Scripture to show that you are sharing truth that will set them free. Take time today to share something you learned in God's Word and how that lesson changed the way you think and live.

Day 31

A Lifestyle of Being Filled with the Word of God: The Word of God Is Living and Active

"For the word of God is living and active, sharper than any two-edged sword, piercing to the division of soul and of spirit, of joints and of marrow, and discerning the thoughts and intentions of the heart."

Hebrews 4:12

EXPERIENCE GOD'S LOVE

We need the Word of God. We need an external indicator of how we are really doing in living out a Christlike life. We need discernment on the "thoughts and intentions" of our own hearts. If we base our progress simply on our own opinion of how well we think we are doing, many times we can settle for far less than what God intends.

Romans 12:2 states, "Do not be conformed to this world, but be transformed by the renewal of your mind, that by testing you may discern what is the will of God, what is good and acceptable and perfect." Change starts in our minds, then moves to our speech, then to our actions. This is true whether the change is positive or negative. If we begin to believe a lie in our minds, that lie will begin to be expressed through our speech and eventually through our actions. If we believe the truth, that truth will come out through our speech and ultimately transform our actions. From this, we can see just how important it is that we fill ourselves with the truth of God's Word.

It is one thing to read the Word of God. It is another to actually apply it. All too often we read God's Word without immediate application. For example, "Give thanks in all circumstances" (1 Thessalonians 5:18); "Do not be anxious about anything" (Philippians 4:6); "Love your enemies" (Matthew 5:44). When we move from reading the Word of God as a nice intellectual concept to taking it as God's Word for us right now, transformation occurs.

There are a variety of ways we may choose to fill ourselves with the truth of God's Word. We may read large quantities of Scripture, we may listen to an audio Bible, or we may meditate on a single verse or even a single word. However we choose to consume God's Word, may we always look to apply it to our lives right now. As we do, we will see it coming in as a sword to cut away everything that is not of God, and at the same time strengthening us to choose God's "good and acceptable and perfect" will (Romans 12:2).

A lifestyle of being filled with God's Word is essential to remaining deeply connected to Christ.

Father, I thank you for your Word. I acknowledge that I need your Word to come in and cut away from me the things that are not of you and to strengthen me to choose your will. Show me how you want me to fill my life with your Word. (Pause and allow Him to speak to you about this.)

EXPRESS GOD'S LOVE

The Word of God doesn't contain any loopholes—it is clear and straightforward. Therefore, if God says, "Do it," then go do it without adding or taking away from whatever it is that He commanded. There are no excuses or justifications to disobey. God knows every detail, every thought, all the intentions and attitudes in which you do things, and if you do them wholeheartedly or half-heartedly. This is good news if you are always giving Him your very best but are afraid of failing. The Holy Spirit will take your best and do the rest; He equips you and bears the fruit.

Prayer: Lord, thank you for your Word. Thank you that I do not have to guess what you want or what will delight your heart. Thank you for clear instructions and boundaries so that I can live a safe and fulfilling life, completing through your Spirit all that you would have me do. Search me and cut away anything that is not pleasing to you.

Care: One of the greatest gifts you could ever give someone is a Bible and some of your time to sit down and read or discuss it with them. Consider doing that today or this week. There are also organizations you can donate to so that they can send Bibles to people who cannot afford them and to people who live in places that don't have access to them. Consider sending the gift of God's Word to someone you've never met.

Share: I (Kathy) was very surprised one evening to have people who do not believe that Jesus is the Son of God engage me in a deep discussion about what He taught. They knew the Scriptures well, and they wanted to know why Jesus taught humility, generosity, unity, forgiveness, and love but they often saw Christians disobeying or even doing the opposite of what Jesus taught. It was a heartbreaking question that provided the opportunity to share how we are imperfect people in the process of learning to live out Christ's love and message. We should always seek to love well, not look for loopholes to try to justify our pride and preferences. Are you close to a Christian friend or family member who is trying to live a "loophole life"? They might think they can base their disobedience on some exception they misquoted or misunderstood in Scripture, but God sees through them to the sin. Humbly share with them about a time in your life when you knowingly disobeyed Jesus, and then lovingly encourage them to search their hearts and their Bibles to get back on track.

Day 32

A Lifestyle of Prayer and Intercession: Power in the Prayer of the Righteous

The prayer of a righteous person has great power as it is working. Elijah was a man with a nature like ours, and he prayed fervently that it might not rain, and for three years and six months it did not rain on the earth. Then he prayed again, and heaven gave rain, and the earth bore its fruit.

James 5:16–18

EXPERIENCE GOD'S LOVE

The power of prayer is the power of God. God merely spoke and the heavens and the earth were created (Genesis 1). His power is literally unlimited. Therefore, there is no limit to what can be accomplished as we humble ourselves in prayer.

Why does it appear that evil is prevailing in so many areas of the earth? Could it be in part because of the prayerlessness of God's people? God has appointed us as His ambassadors on the earth. We are to be the salt and the light of the world. If darkness is prevailing, then the light is not shining as God intended.

The pages of history are filled with men, women, and children who prayed much, believed for much, and brought about great victories in the spiritual and physical realms. There are Christ followers who through their faithfulness in prayer caused wars to cease, famines to abate, disease to flee, and whole people groups to come to faith in Jesus Christ.

Do you want to be a part of changing the course of history? Ask the Spirit of God to shape you into a person of prayer. Elijah was a person just like us, yet through his surrendered prayer life, look what God was able to accomplish.

God is the same yesterday, today, and forever. Could God not answer your prayers regarding the challenges you are facing personally, in your family relationships and in your sphere of influence? Could God not use your life just as He has used others, to win whole people groups to Himself through your faithful prayers?

A lifestyle of prayer and intercession is essential to remaining deeply connected to Christ.

Father, I ask you to place a deep desire in my heart to lay hold of the power that is available to me in prayer. Teach me to become a person of prayer, so that I may be effective in advancing your purposes on the earth. (Continue to pray as God's Spirit leads you.)

EXPRESS GOD'S LOVE

Countless books have been written on prayer—great books to teach you how to pray, ways to pray, and battling the enemy in prayer. The greatest things you can do to know and grow in Jesus are to pray and study the Bible. In order to be a powerful prayer warrior, you have to realize with your whole heart and mind who it is that you are talking to. Jesus' death and resurrection have given us access to the throne room of Almighty God—never take that lightly or enter flippantly. You are praying to the ultimate power and love that exists! He is not limited in any way, and He will never give you something that will hurt you or allow you to sin. Abiding in His Word will equip you to pray in His will.

Prayer: Lord, I want to quiet my heart and mind and come humbly to your throne. Thank you for always hearing my prayers. Teach me to pray what is on your heart. Holy Spirit, give me the words when I don't even know what to say. Stay on my mind, that I might talk with you and give you thanks and praise throughout the day.

Care: One of the most kindhearted ways you can care for someone is to pray for them aloud so that they hear your prayer. There is encouragement and power in our prayers; our words rise to the ears of God, and He heals their broken and wounded places or inspires them to press on, feeling appreciated and honored by you taking them to the feet of Jesus. Practice praying aloud so that you become more and more comfortable praying for others often. Pray for someone today.

⛅ **Share:** Your prayers don't "bother" God, you can't mess up prayer, and you won't be struck by lightning if you say the wrong thing or don't know what to say. Think about a parent who loves to hear their baby talk or get a phone call from their child away at college; it excites their heart. Now think about your heavenly Father who gave you life and sustains it every minute in great provision and protection; God loves hearing your prayers. Share this with someone who thinks their prayers don't matter or that their issue is too small "compared to other people's problems."

A Lifestyle of Prayer and Intercession: Praying the Will of God

And this is the confidence that we have toward him, that if we ask anything according to his will he hears us. And if we know that he hears us in whatever we ask, we know that we have the requests that we have asked of him.

1 John 5:14–15

EXPERIENCE GOD'S LOVE

A trained sniper and an untrained teenage boy are target shooting. The trained rifleman is given a small handgun; the teenage boy is given an assault rifle. The target is placed three hundred yards away, and they are told to begin shooting. The bell sounds, and the inexperienced boy starts wildly firing round after round. When he is out of ammunition, the target is checked, and not a single bullet has hit anywhere on it. The trained rifleman steps up, pauses for a moment, and then fires a single shot and puts his gun down. As they check the target, they see a single bullet hole, right in the center of the target.

When it comes to prayer, which of these two do you resemble the most? Which of these do you want to be like?

For prayer to be effective, it must be in alignment with the will of God. Therefore, rather than coming to God and listing all the things that we think should happen, we need to learn to wait long enough to hear the heart of God. In fact, the definition of the word *prayer* is an exchange of our will and desires for God's will and desires. As we engage in this type of prayer, we can be absolutely confident that God hears us. God's promise to us is that, "if we know that he hears us in whatever we ask, we know that we have the requests that we have asked of him." (1 John 5:15)

Effective prayer is praying out the will of God and being a part of seeing God's purposes advance in the earth. Let's be done with machine-gun prayer that fails to hit the mark. Instead, allow God's Spirit to mold you into a trained prayer warrior: someone who has learned to wait on God, hear His will, and then hit the target every time. Jesus said, "By this my Father is glorified, that you bear much fruit and so prove to be my disciples" (John 15:8). A lifestyle of prayer and intercession is essential to bearing much fruit.

Father, I thank you that you have made a way to have a powerful and effective prayer life. Teach me to wait on you. Teach me to discern your will. Teach me to pray in faith, believing that I have what I ask for when I ask according to your will. I thank you in advance for the fruit that will come through our times of prayer.

EXPRESS GOD'S LOVE

Abiding in God's Word is part of learning God's will, as well as knowing God through your relationship and experiences. God's will is not a guessing game or a moving target—God is the same yesterday, today, and forever. He does not change, and His thoughts, attributes, love, commands, and promises never change. It will never be His will for you to sin or harm yourself. His will is love. He does not will anyone to go to hell; He desires all to come to repentance, that none may perish (2 Peter 3:9). He wills that we worship and glorify Him alone. Knowing God enables us to live and pray right on target with God's heart and purposes.

Prayer: Lord, I desire to pray and do your will. I want my prayers to be fervent and effective, to delight your heart and move your hands. Break my heart for what breaks your heart, and help me not to just shake my fist at injustice but to lend a hand to make things right.

Care: Prayer walking is a great way to cover your neighborhood, campus, workplace, or other areas in prayer. This is especially effective in areas where crime is a problem or if there is a business that exploits people or a place where harm was done and healing needs to take place. Know the needs, the strongholds, and the people who live, work, learn, or come and go from the place you are praying over. Pray for their salvation and for God to draw them near. In the mighty name and blood of Jesus, tell the enemy to get out and stay out. Pray God's presence there, invite the Holy Spirit to fill the atmosphere. Pray at desks and in locker rooms, break rooms, parking lots, offices, and every other part of the building, inside and out.

♻ **Share:** Have you ever thought about what the world would look like if God answered every single one of your prayers today? How would your life, family, city, friends, nation, and the world be different if all your prayers were immediately answered? I am not talking about wide net-casting prayers like "Bless everyone," but your specific, cried-out prayers from your heart to God's. Does this make you want to pray differently? Share with someone today that God hears and answers our prayers. Share a recent prayer that God answered in an amazing but different way than you expected.

Day 34

A Lifestyle of Accountability and Mutual Submission: Encourage One Another Daily

Encourage one another daily, as long as it is called "Today,"
so that none of you may be hardened by sin's deceitfulness.

Hebrews 3:13 NIV

EXPERIENCE GOD'S LOVE

Several years ago, I (Chris) experienced a deep woundedness due to various things that happened at the local congregation we were attending. Though I knew all the right Christian things I should do (forgive, pray for them, bless, etc.), I couldn't seem to overcome the woundedness that had formed in my heart. I allowed isolation from other believers, distance from regular corporate fellowship, and eventually started struggling with areas of sin I had not faced in years.

By God's grace, I had a realization that a life that is truly pleasing to God cannot be lived in isolation. No matter how spiritually strong we may believe ourselves to be, we cannot live out the life God has called us to apart from other brothers and sisters in Christ. We were made for fellowship, with God and with each other.

How about you? Do you have at least one or two other people in your life who are sincerely seeking Jesus and with whom you are totally open and honest about your true spiritual state? Have you prioritized these relationships to the degree that you have a regular schedule to meet, share hearts, and pray together?

A lifestyle of accountability and mutual submission with other Christ followers is essential to remaining deeply connected to Christ. If this type of relationship is not yet in place in your life, begin to ask God to show you at least one or two people whom you can begin to connect with at a deeper level. Allow His Spirit to produce a willingness in your heart to make whatever lifestyle adjustments may be necessary to make this happen.

Father, I choose to thank you that you have made it so that I cannot live out what you have called me to without being in relationship with others. I ask for your forgiveness for times when I have sought to live the Christian life on my own. Today I acknowledge my need for others, and I specifically ask that you reveal to me those whom you desire me to build a deeper relationship with, so that we can strengthen each other. (Take a moment to write down the names of anyone who God places on your heart related to this deeper fellowship.)

EXPRESS GOD'S LOVE

How do you feel when someone says to you, "You are such an encouragement!"? You feel encouraged for encouraging them—you were trying to bless them and then got blessed right back. Encouragement is free, and you can give it all day long and still have plenty to give the next day. Encouragement can come in the form of comfort, a compliment, an instruction, or an exhortation. Sometimes encouragement looks like just being present in a circumstance where someone doesn't want to be alone.

Prayer: Lord, thank you for the people and blessings you have put in my path to encourage me. Help me to make it a habit to encourage others, but I especially want to encourage others in their relationship with you. Prompt me to minister to others in times of pain and to celebrate in times of gain. Encourage me, Holy Spirit, so that I can encourage others with your love and kindness.

Care: You can encourage people with your words and by making their living or work environment better. Is there a neighborhood, park, school, or ball field that could use some cleaning up, fixing up, or fresh paint? Could you gather a group for a Saturday or two to make life safer and more beautiful? Look around some areas of your community or talk with the mayor, principals, or police to find out what areas could use some care and encouragement. Collaborate with other churches or organizations to exhibit unity in the body of Christ and get more done.

Work with one another on projects and celebrate together as you love your community together.

⌂ **Share:** Encouraging others also means steering them in the right direction. The word *accountability* may not be popular, but it is necessary to help fight temptation or to accomplish something that we are striving for or wanting to change in our lives. Share with a trusted friend something that you desire to change or grow or something you struggle with; ask them to pray for you and then privately ask you about it on a weekly basis. Ask them if there is anything you can pray about for them. Encourage one another often. Look for someone who looks like they need encouraging, and offer to listen and pray for them.

Day 35

A Lifestyle of Accountability and Mutual Submission: Iron Sharpens Iron

Iron sharpens iron, and one man sharpens another.

Proverbs 27:17

EXPERIENCE GOD'S LOVE

The Redwoods in Northern California are some of the largest trees in the world. Imagine a tree more than two hundred feet tall and twenty feet wide. Now imagine someone handing you a dull ax and an ax-sharpening tool, then telling you, "You have three hours to chop this down." Would you start striking the tree immediately in order to begin making progress as quickly as possible, or would you spend your initial time sharpening the ax so that every swing at the tree was much more productive?

After my (Chris') realization of the need for fellowship with other believers, I not only started to reconnect with a local congregation, but I also started to look for deeper fellowship opportunities in many different venues (work, community, etc.). I can tell you that the regular interaction I have with my fellow Christ followers is one of the greatest joys of my life. When I am down, they are there to strengthen and uplift me. At other times, they are facing difficulties and I watch as the Holy Spirit uses me to turn their eyes back to God and restore them.

Everyone needs deep and real relationships with other followers of Christ. We will never get so spiritually mature that we outgrow this need for iron-sharpening-iron relationships. I don't know your situation or the obstacles that might seek to hinder you from establishing this type of relationship, but God does. He is more than able to break through whatever hindrances may be there.

A lifestyle of accountability and mutual submission with other Christ followers is essential to remaining deeply connected to Christ. Let's read Hebrews 10:24–25 and then pray into this: "Let us consider how to stir up one another to love and good works, not neglecting to meet together, as is the habit of some, but encouraging one another, and all the more as you see the Day drawing near."

Father, I thank you that you already know those whom you intend to be a part of stirring me up toward love and good works. I ask for your forgiveness for the times when I have neglected to meet with others in this way. I choose to surrender myself to you and ask that you remove every hindrance to a life of deep connection to others. Remove my pride. Remove my fears of rejection. I choose to trust you with this, and I look forward to establishing relationships with those whom you lead me to connect with. (Continue to pray about the specific people who God would have you reach out to, to form this type of deeper relationship. Be proactive to take the first step toward meeting with them on a regular basis.)

EXPRESS GOD'S LOVE

We often live life in response to what has been done to us or for us. We respond in appreciation or reciprocate when someone is kind or generous toward us. We are also prone to retaliate when someone is cruel. Remember your childhood excuse, "He ____ me first" (fill in the blank: hit, hurt, pushed, etc.). Our lives should be focused on the fact that Jesus loved us first. Our response should be to return His love to Him and reflect His love to others. What gifts, talents, and knowledge do you have that could benefit someone else? How can you be used by God as the iron that sharpens someone else today? Who do you go to when you need some "sharpening"? Thank God for them today.

Prayer: Lord, thank you for loving me first. Even when I was far from you, your love drew me to you and covered my sin so that I could respond by loving you in return. Open my eyes, mind, heart, and hands to reflect your love to others. Pour your love through me like living water—let it be a fountain that saturates people in your presence for your glory and purposes.

Care: Let love spill out of the church doors to schools where students and teachers have ongoing needs for volunteers and resources. Go visit the principal and ask what is needed: a campus cleanup day, food for students and families who go hungry over the weekend and on holidays, school supplies, warm clothing, tutors, after-school clubs, and opportunities to learn and serve; the list goes on and on. Work with your neighbors or local churches to care for your local schools; it will make remarkable differences in the near and distant future.

⛅ **Share:** It can be uncomfortable to be transparent with someone and trust them in a deepening relationship, but we were made for relationship. Fellow Christians were meant to help us get through life, to encourage and love one another. We should share wisdom and walk through life with close friends who pray together and stick together. Be the kind of Christian who offers that kind of iron-sharpens-iron friendship. Be willing to use the education and experiences you have been given to connect or provide for people who need to know that Christ and His people care.

Section Five

THE FRUIT OF GOD'S LOVE

By this we know love, that he laid down his life for us, and we ought to lay down our lives for the brothers. But if anyone has the world's goods and sees his brother in need, yet closes his heart against him, how does God's love abide in him? Little children, let us not love in word or talk but in deed and in truth.

1 John 3:16–18

The fruit of a life filled with the love of God results in action and not mere talk. As we are immersing ourselves in the love of God, we should expect to see opportunities to share Christ take place all around us. We should expect to experience a renewed hunger and desire to take the time to disciple those whom God brings into our lives. Ultimately, we should see His unconditional love so utterly consume us that we have His heart for our family, our friends, and even those who are our enemies.

During the last five days of the devotional, we want to look at the fruit we should expect to see, so that if we are not seeing this take place, we will cry out to God for this to become a reality in our lives. He desires our lives to bear "much fruit" (John 15:8). He has said that the "fruit of the Spirit is love" (Galatians 5:22).

As we surrender ourselves completely to Him and trust Him, and as we learn to use the spiritual keys He has given us, this fruit should be flowing in and through us continually.

Father, I thank you that you desire my life to bear much fruit for your glory. As I examine the fruit that you desire from my life, I ask that you work your love even deeper in my heart today. Thank you for giving me the privilege of co-laboring with you to see lives transformed into your image.

Day 36

A Lifestyle of Effective Evangelism: Ambassadors for Christ

In Christ God was reconciling the world to himself, not count-
ing their trespasses against them, and entrusting to us the
message of reconciliation. Therefore, we are ambassadors
for Christ, God making his appeal through us. We implore
you on behalf of Christ, be reconciled to God.

2 Corinthians 5:19–20

EXPERIENCE GOD'S LOVE

I (Chis) was on the pastoral staff of a local church, and our church office was positioned in a downtown area where there was a large homeless population. I had a desire to make an impact in their lives, but I was not sure how. During this time, God's Spirit led me to take hours alone with Him every day. I started to be so filled with His love and compassion for the broken lives around me that I was compelled to go out into the streets and simply offer to pray for people.

Over time, this became a lifestyle. I would spend an extended time being filled with His love in prayer, worship, and the Word of God. Then His Spirit would lead me out among the broken and hurting souls in that street community. Over time, others in the congregation also started to be burdened to proactively serve and share the gospel with those around them. We witnessed God impact many lives that had not experienced being authentically loved before. This ministry was birthed out of simply taking extended time to touch the heart of God.

We have all been called to be God's ambassadors, His emissaries and representatives to the world. How can we properly represent Him if we haven't spent the necessary time to get to know His heart?

When we take the time to be filled with the love of God, loving others flows supernaturally. When God's love for others consumes us, evangelism becomes as natural as breathing air. Without even thinking about it, our love for the Savior starts to pour through us to everyone He brings across our path.

Have you been experiencing God's heart for the lost? Do you desire to have an increased hunger to see souls brought into Christ's kingdom? Ask God to fill you with His love to such a degree that your heart begins to break for the things that break His heart. He has told us that He "desires all people to be saved and to come to the knowledge of the truth" (1 Timothy 2:4). Allow His heart to become your heart today.

Father, I desire to have a revelation of your heart for those who do not yet know you. Give me your heart for them. Grant me your compassion so that I may love lost souls the way that you do. Empower me now to spread your good news to all those you desire.

EXPRESS GOD'S LOVE

An ambassador is a person who is sent from one country to another to represent their home country's people, government, and interests while developing relationships with their host country. As a Christian, you are Christ's ambassador. Your citizenship is in God's kingdom, but you have been sent here to represent Jesus, to support and encourage your fellow citizens, and to bring peace and prosperity. Think about that as you go through your day: you are representing the kingdom and the King. Sin puts us at war with God, but when we share the message of Jesus, we are offering an eternal "peace treaty." Jesus offers life more abundant, eternal prosperity, and earthly blessings that we could and should count every day. Realize the importance of your role as Christ's ambassador and go share and serve Him well.

👤 **Prayer:** Lord, thank you for the peace and joy of knowing that my eternal citizenship is with you in your kingdom. I rejoice that my name is written in the Lamb's book of life (Revelation 21:27). I want to represent you well, for people to know your love, goodness, authority, and power from my life and testimony. Let this be my first priority, to live as your ambassador and to love your people and increase your kingdom.

❤️ **Care:** Think about the people who represent you: congressmen, city councils, mayors, governors, state legislators, boards, and more. They cannot represent you well if they do not know you, yet so many people have never met any of these people. Do you know their names? Pray for them, their families, their positions, and their staff. Pray protection and wisdom over them, and ask God to speak clearly into their lives so that their decisions and actions are pleasing and glorifying to Him. Write them a letter thanking them for their service and let them know that you are praying for them.

♻ **Share:** We rely on God's protection with every breath and second of the day. He created and sustains us and we would perish without him. His protection gives you courage and comfort, and fear vanishes when we focus on our great God watching over us. Share this with someone who seems to worry or be fearful frequently. Let them know that God watching over them is like a parent watching their new baby sleep; He just can't take His eyes off you.

Day 37

Developing a Lifestyle
of Effective Discipleship

What you have learned and received and heard and seen in me—practice these things, and the God of peace will be with you.

Philippians 4:9

EXPERIENCE GOD'S LOVE

Paul was one of the greatest evangelists who has ever lived. Largely on foot, he traveled the nations winning souls to Christ wherever he went. Yet he understood the deep and essential value of discipleship. Everywhere he went, he not only won souls into the kingdom, but he also took the time to disciple them in God's ways. Our love for others should go beyond merely seeing people come to Christ, carrying on into a willingness to lay down our lives for them to be conformed into the image of Jesus.

Sadly, much of the church seems to have lost sight of the value of life-on-life discipleship. In the structure of many congregations, a large weekly service, and in some cases a midweek teaching time, have replaced the daily meeting together in the temple and houses that took place in the early church (Acts 2:46). Even in areas where small groups exist, how many believers are so filled with God's love that they are willing to make the time investment to pour their lives into others? How many are willing to fight through the obstacles that come and keep loving others?

Many marriages and families are suffering from a lack of discipleship. The statistics in many nations show a sad reality taking place in Christian homes. In many areas of the world, the people of God have allowed the world's belief system to become the main discipler of the younger generation. As television, film, and the internet consume the lives of many Christian families, is it any wonder that vast swaths of those raised in Christian homes are choosing to reject Christ? Where is the love of Christ that would compel us to take the time to disciple our families? Where is the daily, life-on-life instruction in what it means to really know God and walk in His ways?

Discipleship should be a centerpiece in our lives, our families, and whatever sphere of influence that God has entrusted to us. Jesus told us to go and make "disciples," not merely converts (Matthew 28:19). This is the Great Commission. Today, what is God's Spirit saying to you? Are there any practical lifestyle adjustments that you need to make for discipleship to become more a part of your life?

Father, I thank you that the discipleship of the nations is deeply on your heart. I believe that this begins with me and with the lives of those whom you have placed around me. Show me how you would have me become more deeply engaged in pouring my life into others. (Take time to wait and hear His reply. Ask Him about specific people and specific ways He would have you be willing to pour your life into others.)

EXPRESS GOD'S LOVE

My (Kathy's) daughter Emily loves to *play* the piano, but she had to learn to love to *practice*. There is a big difference in playing and practicing; you play songs that are easy or familiar without replaying the sections where you stumble. Playing is leisurely but practice is a different ballgame. When you practice, you polish songs you already know as well as dive into new songs that challenge you and take more work. If we do not practice, we forget what we have learned and we do not expand our talent. This is true for everything in life: relationships, work, school, and living and expressing the love and message of Jesus. Don't get discouraged, practice.

Prayer: Lord, I know there have been so many times you've had to re-teach me because I did not put into practice the lessons you taught me. I don't want to go through the pain of relearning hard lessons; help me to put them into practice in my everyday life so that they become a natural part of my character. I am your disciple; teach me, grow me, that I might bear much fruit for your glory.

Care: Being a pastor, especially for the average size church of 150 people or less, is not an easy job. Some would think, *How hard can it be to write a sermon each week and shake some hands?* But it is so much more than that! A pastor rushes to the side of their congregation in times of personal, family, and community crises and celebrations. They are often criticized more than they are appreciated, and they are expected to run the business side of the church as well as the spiritual, usually on a small budget and smaller staff. The only harder job is to be the pastor's wife. Show appreciation to your pastor and his wife this week. Write them a letter telling them how they impact your life, give them a gift, or take them out for a meal. Pastors give so much care; put into practice caring for yours.

♻ **Share:** Do you know someone who makes the same mistake over and over again? They suffer the hard consequences and you think they learned their lesson, only to watch them fall, or run, back into trouble. Share Christ's message of love and hope with them today. With a gentle tone and lovingkindness, offer to journey with them to put into practice the hard lessons that they have endured so they do not suffer any longer.

Unconditional Love:
It Begins with Receiving

There is therefore now no condemnation for those who are in Christ Jesus. For the law of the Spirit of life has set you free in Christ Jesus from the law of sin and death.

Romans 8:1–2

EXPERIENCE GOD'S LOVE

We have addressed this numerous times throughout the forty days, but loving others unconditionally has to begin in our own hearts. We simply cannot give to others what we have not first received from God. God wants us to know that we are loved unconditionally, that He has removed condemnation from us through the shed blood of Jesus Christ. We are justified and made whole again solely and only thorough the finished work of Jesus.

We can know these things intellectually, yet still fail to walk in them as a daily reality. We desperately need the Spirit of God to take the truth of God and reveal it to us so that we know that we know that we are loved.

Clearly God's love for us cannot be based on our emotions. If we base God's love for us on our emotions, we would be on a constant roller coaster, feeling loved one day and unloved the next.

Instead, we must learn to take God at His Word. He is the one who has said, "I have loved you with an everlasting love" (Jeremiah 31:3). He is the one who has said that He "will never leave you nor forsake you" (Deuteronomy 31:6 NIV). We must come to a maturity in our faith where we simply accept what He has said about us as the truth and walk in it as our daily inheritance as His children.

This is not arrogance; it is taking God at His Word. This simple yet profound practice exchanges our up-and-down emotions for the solid rock of the Word of God, which will never change. Allow God's Spirit to teach you to make this exchange of your emotions for His eternal truth, and you will never be the same. A lifestyle of unconditional love for others begins by receiving God's unconditional love for you.

Father, I thank you that you love me unconditionally. I thank you that this is based on your Word, which will never change. Teach me to walk in the full assurance of your love for me in every circumstance so that I am prepared to extend unconditional love to others.

EXPRESS GOD'S LOVE

In Christ, there is no *condemnation*, a legal word noting guilt and being condemned to punishment. In Christ's love and forgiveness, all disapproving or negative thoughts toward others or yourself should be washed away and replaced with the biblical truth of Christ's affection and authority. Thoughts are powerful; the mind controls the brain and the brain controls the body. What do you find yourself thinking about most? Are you a dreamer or a dreader? Do you think about how wonderful things can be, how to improve life for yourself and others, and are your dreams positive and happy, or do you tend to think worse-case scenario? Do you think negative thoughts about yourself? Your thoughts can actually affect your physical and spiritual health and heart. Scripture tells us to think life-giving, loving thoughts.

👤 **Prayer:** Lord, thank you for saving me, that I am not condemned. I want to keep my mind on you. There is nothing and no one more excellent and worthy of praise than you and your ways, your promises and love. Help me to remember that every person is made in your image and therefore worthy of pure and honorable thoughts. Help me to keep my mind closed to satan and to negative thoughts about myself, my circumstances, or others.

❤ **Care:** Your words can change someone's day, and they just might change someone's life. People are plagued with insecurities, fears, and negative thoughts. Your positive, kind, and complementary words encouraging them, pointing out their strengths, and expressing gratitude can drown out the negative thoughts that keep them from reaching their destiny. People who make mistakes need to hear about forgiveness and clean slates; people who have been told they were a mistake or will never amount to anything need to hear that they were included in God's plan before there was time. Consider writing letters to people in prison, becoming a tutor, or spending time with someone who has made hurtful choices and is living out the consequences. Tell them about the second chance Jesus offers.

⬆ **Share:** Most people think negative thoughts about themselves. Even people who seem conceited have insecurity issues and often cover them up by trying to tell everyone how great they are. Share with someone today how God sees them—they are His beautiful, gifted creation that He loves so much that He was willing to send His Son to die for them. Let them know how precious and valuable they are to God. Make sure you believe this for yourself as well.

Unconditional Love:
Loving Our Families

Everyone who believes that Jesus is the Christ has been born of God, and everyone who loves the Father loves whoever has been born of him.

1 John 5:1

EXPERIENCE GOD'S LOVE

Unconditional love is supposed to be the hallmark of the people of God. As we have already stated, this starts with believing that God loves us unconditionally. From there, God's love is to flow through us to "whoever has been born of him" (1 John 5:1).

If you have been born of God's Spirit, you now have two families. You have your biological family members, and you have your spiritual family members. Through the blood of Jesus Christ, we have literally become family with everyone who has been born of God's Spirit. We are called by God to love our family. No matter who they are or what they may have done to us.

Has unconditional love been the hallmark of your relationships with your biological family? How about the relationships within your local congregation? Would you say that you see the majority of those around you preferring others above themselves, turning the other cheek, and going the extra mile?

If not, this does not give us permission to start pointing fingers at others. Instead, God's solution has always been for us to model and mentor the difference. Let me explain. If we see a lack of unconditional love in our physical or spiritual family, is it going to really change things if we go to them in anger and tell them that they have failed us? There is certainly an important place for speaking the truth in love, but why not begin with a season of self-evaluation? Ask God, "Am I truly preferring the members of my family above myself? If not, what would you have me change?"

Take a moment and ask God these two simple questions. Allow Him to bring to your attention any member of your biological or spiritual family with whom there is a need for greater love on your part.

The truth is, God intends for you to be part of His solution to the lack of love in the earth. He can use you to be the catalyst for unconditional love springing up in your family, in your local congregation, and beyond. It begins with you. Allow God to work a deeper, more unconditional love in your own heart for those around you. Then you will be in position to model this love to others.

Father, I thank you that you love all those in my physical and spiritual family. I desire to fulfill your Word by loving them as you love them. Forgive me for every way I have held on to unforgiveness from past hurtful experiences that have hindered me from loving them as you have asked me to. Today, I believe you to fill me with your love for all my family members. I thank you in advance for the fruit that you will bring from this.

EXPRESS GOD'S LOVE

Today's verse from 1 John expands on John's writing in John 3, where Jesus talked with Nicodemus, who was caught in the conundrum of being a highly respected and influential religious leader while also realizing the significance of Jesus' teachings. Nicodemus went to ask Jesus questions in the cover of darkness, possibly to avoid the crowds or maybe to avoid the harassment from his peers who had their hearts set on killing Jesus. This conversation gave us the most noted and quoted Bible verse as Jesus answered Nicodemus' question, "How can a man be born again?" Jesus said, "For God so loved the world that he gave his one and only Son, that whoever believes in him shall not perish but have eternal life" (John 3:16 NIV).

Prayer: Lord, thank you for listening. Thank you for answering our questions. Thank you for modeling in your lifetime how we can gently and truthfully answer questions that come from the heart of someone who wants to know you more. Thank you for loving me into your family. Thank you for all of the opportunities you give me to go and love others. Thank you for my family and my spiritual family, and help me to love them well.

Care: Who do you go to when you have questions about the Bible or God? Have you ever had anyone make you feel stupid when you were seeking understanding? Have you ever had a peer, coworker, or friend make fun of you for your interest in "religious things"? Jesus' answer was saturated in love and all about love. Love gives. God loved us so much that He gave the most precious gift in all of history to meet a need no other could fulfill. How does love draw you to give? Is there an injustice in this world, in your community, that breaks your heart? Is there a need that you know you could fill, either with some personal sacrifice or by getting a group of people together to meet the need or change the situation? Pray and think about this and then go and give.

⬥ **Share:** Christ's love causes us to share his love; once you experience it, you must go express it. Jesus said, "By this everyone will know that you are my disciples, if you love one another" (John 13:35 NIV). When people ask you why you care, why you give, why you sacrifice for others, always be quick to answer that it is Jesus' love pouring through you. Share Jesus through your love.

Unconditional Love:
Love for Our Enemies

"You have heard that it was said, 'You shall love your neigh-bor and hate your enemy.' But I say to you, Love your enemies and pray for those who persecute you, so that you may be sons of your Father who is in heaven. For he makes his sun rise on the evil and on the good, and sends rain on the just and on the unjust."

Matthew 5:43–45

EXPERIENCE GOD'S LOVE

God loves His enemies. Pause and let this sink in. God fervently and passionately loves all those who hate Him. This kind of love goes beyond our human understanding. We cannot fathom love for a serial killer, a rapist, or a person who abuses their children.

Jesus goes on to say in Matthew 5:46, "If you love those who love you, what reward do you have? Do not even the tax collectors do the same?" He effectively says, "Look, anyone can love those who love them, but as my children, you are called to a much higher standard of love."

We are called to love like God loves. Just the thought of that should leave us trembling. As God's children, we have received

His great love, and He fully expects us to love others in the exact same way that He loves us. And that means even our enemies.

Allow the Holy Spirit to lead you into His love for all of humanity. Picture the person who you believe is the most evil person alive. Do you realize that God loves them unconditionally and desires them to come to know Him? In fact, God loves them with a passion that is greater than your love for those who are closest to you.

"As the heavens are higher than the earth, so are my ways higher than your ways" (Isaiah 55:9). As you allow God to show you the love that He has for all people, you will be transformed. Justifications and excuses for holding on to unforgiveness have to go in the light of His love. You are a child of the God of love. You have been called to love as He loves. He loves His enemies, and you must love yours.

As you really step into the reality of experiencing and expressing His love, there is no telling the difference that your life will make. For it was this same revelation of love that drove our Savior to be willing to lay down His life for His enemies. As we learn to love as God loves, even our enemies can be won to Jesus.

Father, I thank you for inviting me into your life of love. I ask for your forgiveness for the times when I have failed to love my enemies as you desire me to. Today, by your grace, I choose to love those who have sinned against me. I believe you to show me how to walk out this love every day of my life.

EXPRESS GOD'S LOVE

Who are your enemies? Do you really have any enemies? Well, you have one enemy, satan and his fallen army, but as far as people go you really do not have enemies, you only have a mission field. Any person who is far from God and does evil, cruel things is being blinded by satan, held captive in his tricks and traps. You are the warrior who should pray for them. If there is any opportunity, you should live out the tangible love of Jesus toward them. Never turn your back on a person made in the image of God who is headed for eternal torture and separation from God.

👤 **Prayer:** Lord, I pray right now for the people who first crossed my mind as my enemies. I repent for forgetting that they are victims of satan, who comes to steal, kill, and destroy. I beg you to reveal yourself to _____ (fill in a name). Let them know your love; tear off the blinders of the real enemy, and use your people, even me, to share your love and message with them.

❤️ **Care:** If you have treated someone like an enemy, change your attitude and actions toward them beginning today. As a Christ follower, we only push people farther away from Jesus when we judge them or treat them with contempt. Christ loved you first, so now go love them first as He loved you. Pray that God will change their heart as you change your behavior.

⛅ **Share:** Can you believe that this is the final day of the 40 Days of Love? So now what? Well, we go love on day 41, 42, 43, and 99. We love until in the blink of an eye we are absent from the body and present with the Lord. *Forty Days of Love* was meant to help you make love a lifestyle, to see how easy and fulfilling it is to live out a Prayer-Care-Share lifestyle—even to your "enemies." Never stop sharing the love and message of Jesus. You were born to love and live out Christ's love.

Conclusion

I am sure of this, that he who began a good work in you will bring it to completion at the day of Jesus Christ.

Philippians 1:6

To enter into a lifestyle of unconditional love is no small thing. We will have times when we fail and will need to humble ourselves and ask God's forgiveness. It is our fervent hope and desire that as you have meditated on the Scriptures and insights here, that the Spirit of God has convicted you of sin as well as inspired you to believe God for a new life, a life of love that chooses to prefer others above yourself. A life that goes beyond mere lip service to tangible expressions of care for those around you. And a life that shares the good news of Jesus Christ with everyone who God brings into your life. In all this, we trust God's Spirit to complete the good work that He has begun in you.

We are grateful to be a small part of your journey with Jesus. We hope that these 40 Days of Love have been a special time in your relationship with God. We encourage you to continue to use this devotional well beyond the first forty days to reflect on God's love. In time, we trust His Spirit will mold your heart more and more into His image, with the result being great glory to Jesus!

Journeying with you to experience and express the love of God,

Chris Vennetti and Kathy Branzell

• • •

For more information on sharing the 40 Days of Love with others, go to: www.40DaysofLove.net or visit www.Love2020.com.

About the Authors

Chris Vennetti is the co-founder of the "40 Days of Love," an initiative that seeks to empower Christ-followers in a lifestyle of prayer, care, share evangelism. Chris also helps to steward Disciples Nations International, an international missions organization focused on personal, family, and community transformation. Chris and his wife live with their five children in Orlando, Florida.

Kathy Branzell is a speaker, author, National Coordinator of LOVE2020, and has been an active member of the Mission America Coalition since 2000. Kathy began her ministry journey as the founder and president of Fellowship and Christian Encouragement (FACE) for Educators. FACE has grown to over 130,000 public and private school educators who meet and pray in their schools each week. She is also a board member of the National Prayer Committee and a working member of the Board of Directors for The National Day of Prayer. Kathy lives in Atlanta, Georgia, with her husband and is mom to two grown children.

40 DAYS of LOVE

40 DAYS Of Praying, Caring and Sharing the Gospel to **Transform Nations**

40DaysofLove.net

Journey into the
Spirit Empowered Life
A Guide to Personal, Family & Community Transformation

"Journey into the Spirit Empowered Life will help you discover and cultivate a lifestyle that is totally surrendered to Christ, and walks daily in the power of the Holy Spirit."
Dr. Dick Eastman
International President, Every Home for Christ

"As you read this book, I pray that God will speak loudly to you. It is a call to follow Jesus unreservedly with full surrender and to give up what so many of us have held onto for too long."
Milton Monell
Director of Global Prayer, Campus Crusade for Christ

"May the Lord use this teaching to drive us back to scripture in a way that results in Spirit-led, scripture-fed expressions of God's love."
Phil Miglioratti
National Pastors' Prayer Network

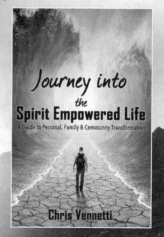

CLT
Christ-Like Lifestyle Training

Go to our website to learn more:
www.CLTonline.net

BECOME THE PERSON GOD CREATED YOU TO BE

What difference would it make at your ministry or business if everyone was:

• Growing in a greater awareness of God's love for them and for those around them.
• Speaking a common language and sharing a common vision.
• Dealing with areas of past woundedness that hinder their ability to love and relate with others.
• Dealing with areas of personal sin (anger, lust, jealousy, appetite, sloth, greed, pride, unbelief) in a way that is constructive and transformative.
• Learning to work together as a team, preferring others above themselves, and leading by serving.
• Walking out a lifestyle of deep intimacy with God that results in effective prayer, evangelism and discipleship.

Would this make a difference? If so, what would you be willing to invest in order to see this take place?

Components of the Christ-Like Lifestyle Training have been endorsed by national leaders, translated into multiple languages, and are being used by ministry leaders in many nations.

Topics Include:

• The Power of One Vessel Prepared by the Master
• Testimonies of Personal & Corporate Transformation
• Becoming Part of God's Solution: Dealing with Our Unfinished Business
• Understanding and Overcoming Woundedness
• Foundation of a Spirit Empowered Life
• Spiritual Keys to Living in Christ-Likeness
• Marriage and Family Transformation
• Establishing Christ's Kingdom in the Workplace

40DaysofLove.net